Advanced
Dowsing
with the
LifeWeaving
System

PROTOCOLS, TECHNIQUES AND TIPS
FOR HEALING YOURSELF AND OTHERS

Carole Conlon, L.Ac.,
Master Integrational Healer

AyniWrite Press
Albuquerque, NM

Carole Conlon/AyniWrite Press
10700 Academy Rd NE #2227
Albuquerque, NM 87111
www.AyniWritePress.com

Edited by Barbara J. Rose
Book Layout ©2013 BookDesignTemplates.com

Ordering Information:
Quantity sales. Special discounts are available on quantity purchases by corporations, associations, and others. For details, contact the publisher at the address above.

Advanced Dowsing with the LifeWeaving System---Protocols, Techniques and Tips for Healing Yourself and Others/ Carole Conlon. —1st ed.
ISBN 978-0-9907550-2-9

The Transmuting Violet Flame Prayer

Holy Father/Mother God, Creator of all that is,
I call on the Law of Forgiveness for myself and all mankind
for all mistakes, mis-qualified energy
and for straying from the Light.
Holy Father/Mother God, Creator of all that is,
blaze through me the Limitless Transmuting Violet Flame,
Thy Sacred Fire,
and Transmute now all impure desire, hard feelings,
wrong concepts, imperfect etheric records,
causes, effects and memories, known or unknown,
in this life time or any other lifetime,
in all dimensions of my subtle body
and physical body.
Keep this flame sustained and all powerfully active.
Replace this karma with pure substance,
power of accomplishment and the divine plan fulfilled.
Charge me with perfect health,
joy,
happiness,
illumination,
love,
wisdom,
power
and abundance
in the name of the Cosmic Christ Vibration.

Amen

Contents

Foreword

It is a joy to introduce Carole Conlon to you today! If you are a healer, I hope this book provides you with more tools to help those around you, and if you are looking for healing, I hope it brings you comfort and peace. Whatever your background may be, I wish you much love and courage.

For as long as I can remember, I have always been fascinated by the world beyond what the human eye can see. Growing up singing in the church choir, faith has always been the central part of my life. Prayer, worship, and service the foundations of my childhood. At 17, I moved to New York City to pursue my acting career, and while my spirit and beliefs were questioned and challenged, they were ultimately strengthened. As I got my start working in theater in New York City, I started to see little miracles, or God winks as I often call them, along the way. People started showing up in my life that I felt I had known before. Doors were opening that had always been closed. I may not have known many people when I started out in the entertainment industry, but I had faith. This faith provided the courage I needed to guide me to where I needed to go. At 19, I moved to Los Angeles and was cast in my first television series called "American Dreams." And a career in film and television that I had dreamed about and worked towards for years began. When I was cast in a series filming in New Mexico, I met Carole Conlon. The steps that led to us meeting were filled with some very marvelous synchronicities.

My first experience in New Mexico was a bit dramatic. My rental car was broken into while I was parked in a church parking lot in the middle of the day. An old phone and bag from work along with some love letters from my boyfriend at the time were taken and a shattered passenger's seat window left behind. I filed a report with the Albuquerque, New Mexico Police Department, and two months later, when I was working in New York City again, received a call. Detective Willoughby from the Albuquerque PD had found my phone. I spoke with the detectives for a few months trying to arrange a time to pick up my belongings, and then, something very interesting happened. I was cast to play a detective on a television series filming in Albuquerque called *In Plain Sight*. This left me befuddled. Befuddled is the best word I can think of to describe the state I was in. How on earth is this possible? What the heck? If life really is a play within a play, this just took it to the next level. How does one get robbed in New Mexico, get a call from detectives in New Mexico about said robbery, and then return to New Mexico to play a detective protecting other people from the same experience. This is amazing. My eyes were wide open. God really does have a plan.

I met Carole during the first few weeks of filming this new series in New Mexico. While talking with a friend about some of these experiences, she suggested I call Carole. With her gentle voice and endless knowledge about the world around us, Carole pulled out a chart and started to check in with me and the people in my life. How are we all connected? What is our mission? A trust developed, and after I returned to Los Angeles, I was cast to play a witch in a television series about past lives, magic, love, and mystery on a show called *Witches of East End*. And so my studies began!

Carole knew this world so well and began to explain her Life-Weaving techniques and years of study and service to me. As a curious human and artist, I asked a thousand questions while I began to explore the world I would be entering on the television series. At the same time, I also watched this work transform relationships in my own life. As I opened to the idea of consciousness and triggers from the past, I was awakened to changes I could make and places in my own heart that needed to be nurtured and loved if I was going to allow for more loving and supportive relationships to enter my life. I would be playing a woman who was just beginning to embrace and step into her power. She was afraid to let go of the identity she had created for herself and become who she was truly meant to be. So we explored how to break free of old patterns and how to embrace the freedom to become our most present and authentic selves.

Whether you are coming to this work with a lifetime of experience, this is your first time to explore, or you just stumbled upon it with curiosity, I am excited about your path ahead. I hope this book encourages you to go within your own soul and trust the quiet whispers and hopes of your heart.

Love and light,

Rachel Boston

Preface

As an acupuncturist, I always tried to identify and treat dis-ease at the root layer, yet I found that patients sometimes returned months later with what seemed to be the same problem. Clearly they had not healed on some level. This led me to start developing the LifeWeaving System. The first chart I created was called PENDU-LUM RESEARCH SOURCING METHOD (PRSM), a diagnostic system that incorporated what I considered to be the best portions of the many healing methods that I had ever studied.

Armed with the PRSM Chart, I began to pendulum for both the root cause of a client's presenting complaint as well as any other problems being affected by that root cause, but eventually I came to see the fallacy of this approach. The pendulum results showed trends from treatment to treatment but mostly clients failed to undergo the dramatic and complete healing I had expected. Also, as I continued to research at deeper levels, I usually found an emotional basis for the physical complaints, thereby resulting in new questions. For instance, (1) how does one treat these emotional issues without winding up in long-term counseling?; (2) what is the actual root level of a dis-ease?; (3) is the root level of a dis-ease in the body, the mind, the emotions or a combination of these? (4) how far down on the causal list should one attempt to treat - the origin of a problem or the most recent symptom?

Due to a personal health challenge in late 1995, I consulted with a practitioner who used a pendulum method called Spiritual Response Therapy (SRT). The result of this session was a vast improvement in both my health and mental outlook. Developed by Robert Detzler, SRT utilizes charts and a pendulum to research and aid spiritual clearing. This personal experience made me realize that the spiritual level of healing was the missing link in my own work: if we are to heal, we must heal on all four levels - the physical, emotional, mental and spiritual. Also, I realized that it was important to focus on what is ready to be healed - not on some special underlying layer.

Over the years, my approach to healing has changed dramatically. I now place emphasis on clearing emotional blockages that lock health problems into the mind, body and/or spirit. I also realize that when using the complete LifeWeaving system with clients, a health problem that already shows up on the physical body level means that in addition to my spiritual approach, a physical approach is often needed for the body.

In looking at healing from a spiritual approach, I also learned to pay attention to a person's dimensional level. The dimension scale used with the LifeWeaving system ranges from 3rd to the 12th, and each has 12 levels called octaves. The Earth has been at the 3rd dimension (length, width and depth) but is now moving through the 4th (time and emotions) to the 5th, the last physical level. Beyond the 5th, our bodies are in spirit form. An advanced spirit is able to operate across both lower and higher levels, has memories and energies that affect the physical body and will respond to life in a much different way than a soul at the lower levels.

I came to realize that whatever the healing method used, a client's beliefs and/or open or closed-mindedness will influence the results. I learned that when using LifeWeaving dowsing on a client with a soul consciousness level hovering in the 3rd to the lower 7th vibrational dimensions, he or she will probably have trouble accepting this healing method and won't experience much change. If the client is at a 7th vibrational dimension or slightly above, results can be quite good. For a client ranging up to the 11th or 12th level of consciousness, the results can be extraordinary!

My specific intent with LifeWeaving is to present a system which incorporates a way to explore and address all body levels. The three key dowsing charts developed for this system allow the practitioner to identify any area or level of the body that is either blocked by, or involved in, a health issue - thus facilitating the client's treatment.

These charts can also be used to identify, research and clear blocking issues that may be affecting all areas of life - business, relationships, pets, etc.

I present the LifeWeaving method as a means to unlock your intuitive mind to all possibilities when working with your own issues or with those of clients. To provide the best help possible, use any dowsed information in combination with observation, other test methods and, especially, common sense.

From The Breath of God's Light,

I AM, I AM, I AM

Carole

LOVE

Acknowledgments

The LifeWeaving system is the result of a long journey of weaving my personal studies with that of many superior and pivotal teachers.

Over 30 years ago, Barbara Wallace first introduced me to pendulum work and started me on this path. Next, Robert Detzler showed me how to take pendulum work to a new level when I studied his method called Spiritual Response Therapy. As I used his pendulum charts and dowsing system, I saw the potential of moving away from traditional dowsing and took the liberty to create my own charts and system. Freedom!

The LifeWeaving charts have gone through many name and content changes during the various stages of development. Each stage got its trial run resulting in even more modifications. During this time, my good friend and LifeWeaving student, Barbara J. Rose, came to my aid by professionally editing manuals and giving me welcome constructive criticism on this body of work.

However, a constant demand for simplification came from another source, friend and student Brian T. Roberts, who pressed for clearer instructions and a simpler form for the method. That led to even more changes and, although we never quite reached true simplicity with the charts, the method became more streamlined.

I do also have to thank my acupuncture patients who stayed with me as my healing approach began turning to more intervention on the emotional and spiritual levels as I incorporated LifeWeaving clearing into sessions along with the needles.

I also thank the many students who have taken the challenge to learn LifeWeaving. Believe me, it has been a challenge to share the body of work and I only hope that I showed enough patience!

And finally I wish to acknowledge the spirits - including Jesus, Metatron, Stephen Hawking, Cecil B. DeMill and The Phantom - who helped develop this body of work by channeling some of this information and process to me.

I AM, I AM, I AM so grateful!

Carole

CHAPTER 1

Introduction to LifeWeaving

Figure 1 LifeWeaving Symbol

The LifeWeaving Process Defined

LifeWeaving, a multidimensional dowsing method, uses special charts to identify and immediately remove emotional blockages that are layered in the body. The clearing process is designed to move a person into a state of neutrality - a place where everything "just is" - without emotional baggage, biases or feelings.

The basic LifeWeaving process is simple. First a question, a situation, a relationship or even an illness is posed and translated into a set of word frequencies by dowsing the charts. These word frequencies are collected and spiraled throughout the body in order to nullify the blocking energy signature. After that energy is cleared, the frequency of unconditional love is infused back through the body to complete the healing.

LifeWeaving is a tool you can use to seek answers, to nourish and enhance your life, and to empower yourself on a daily basis to meet life's "little challenges." Living life from a neutral point of view can enable you to deal with stress more easily and bring great reward.

The Science Behind LifeWeaving

Why does any change occur at all when the LifeWeaving method is applied? First of all words, like colors and sounds, have their own energy. Remember as a small child when your mom or dad yelled at you for doing something bad? You felt that energy! Or if you have ever been near two people who are arguing, you can feel their anger. LifeWeaving precipitates a clearing by using the frequencies of words, essentially a collection of specific sound waves.

Sound waves, created through elastic compression (a rapid pushing together) and rarefaction (a rapid pulling apart) of air molecules, are measured in wavelengths - the distance that one phase of compression and rarefaction travels in a second. These physical waves freely intermix and can be either in or out of phase. In the case of being perfectly 180 degrees out of phase, the sound waves completely nullify each other, resulting in silence.

LifeWeaving relies on this same phenomenon. Through the dowsing process, buried memories of an emotional wound are awakened and moved into the lower conscious mind. Then as the sound frequencies of the dowsed words and energies spiral throughout the body, mind and spirit, those wave patterns invert 180 degrees out of phase with the matching blocking frequencies which are, in turn, nullified. After this type of clearing, emotions, energy, blood or fluids can flow again on the physiological level resulting in an increase of vitality to the area and a decrease of physical pain.

What Can LifeWeaving Help?

Overall, LifeWeaving clearing can have far-ranging effects on people, animals, inanimate objects, health issues, relationships, various life situations or even business decisions.

A beginning LifeWeaver can use this method to do daily work to clear him or herself and, at the same time, experience how this type of clearing can impact life. As confidence in the LifeWeaving process develops, he or she can begin helping family and friends. A skilled LifeWeaver can start with an obvious complaint or symptom and begin to uncover the many layers and threads of times and occurrences that are involved; then can untangle and nullify those influences to help restore energy and return a system to its original, healthy blueprint.

The following are some examples of the different uses for LifeWeaving:

- **Reduce Personal Stress**: As the world energy shifts into the 5th dimension, more and more buried emotional blockages are surfacing causing both physical and emotional stress. **LifeWeaving** quickly finds and effectively releases these blockages, helping a person to remain clear and in a neutral state of mind - both of which help stressful situations.

- **Health Applications**: By clearing up blocked energy levels, **LifeWeaving** allows for faster and more complete healing. However, since this method begins working from a spiritual level and moves downwards towards into the physical, combining it with a physical healing approach is even better.

  Ways to use **LifeWeaving** include:

o **Diagnosis and Treatment:** By **LifeWeaving** you can identify subconscious reasons a person has for needing to experience pain or other symptoms, and then clear these reasons by going to and releasing the root cause. Also, **LifeWeaving** can be applied to researching and clearing the many contributing aspects of a problem such as its origin, affected areas of the body, being resistant to healing, etc.

o **Moving Past a Healing Plateau:** If you hit a plateau while receiving hands-on care or counseling, the **LifeWeaving** method seamlessly integrates with, and enhances the effects of, these and any other treatment approaches by finding and removing deep-seated emotional blockages to healing. Usually one or two **LifeWeaving** sessions can release any subconscious resistance to healing. A person can then move beyond the plateau and resume shifting into wellness.

o **Clearing Trauma:** In trauma cases, **LifeWeaving** can be used to research and clear the injured or any other persons, such as family members or rescuers, affected by an incident. **LifeWeaving** removes trauma imprints that form at the time of an accident - imprints that can affect those involved for many years or lifetimes to come. Post-traumatic stress falls into this category.

▪ **Relationship Issues:** Throughout our lives, we are shown examples of emotional wounds we carry that need to be healed. Often as not, these issues come to us in the form of a mirror - *e.g.,* that person in our life who drives us crazy! Once we have learned the lesson and released the blocked energy, the mirror is no longer needed so the carrier of the message either disappears from our life or suddenly changes for the better. How nice is that? Once relationship issues have been cleared of any past emotional blocks through **LifeWeaving**, the parties involved will be able to either create a renewed positive connection or to separate without regret.

A few examples of relationship clearing include:

- o Couples counseling

- o Identifying and clearing sources of conflict with others

- o Helping a job applicant decide if he or she would fit in with other employees, the business and the owner

- o Helping a business owner decide if an applicant should be hired

- o Helping a person decide with whom to spend more energy on when online dating

- **Interpreting and Clearing Animal Behavior**: LifeWeaving dowsing research can help to put a label to the various actions, emotions and reactions of an animal, thus giving the owner a better understanding of the problem and how to help.

For example, **LifeWeaving** was effectively used to pinpoint and clear the reasons why a horse always shied when approaching the open end of a show ring. **LifeWeaving** was also used by dowsing words and archetypes to see how a horse identified its previous owners and trainers.

LifeWeaving was also used to uncover the story of what had happened to make a young cat suddenly lose its confidence and become fearful of its environment.

Setting the Metaphysical Stage

Figure 2 Ascension Energy

Now Entering the 7th Golden Age

Planet Earth is currently accelerating into the 5th dimension and the "Seventh Golden Age" - the beginning of 1000 years of peace, prosperity and abundance. Because of this planetary shift, our own vibrational frequencies and soul consciousness levels are rising as our bodies and spirits also try to make the change into a world of light and crystalline-based life. However, our successful transition can be slowed or blocked if our dense physical bodies cannot hold the light - a problem caused by underlying emotional blockages. Therefore the main focus now of any effective healing method must be to address underlying emotions rather than to just treat symptoms. Without releasing these limiting blocks, the physical body cannot easily shift and absolute healing cannot take place. To complement the change, rapid identification and clearing methods that use intuition, pendulum and charts, tapping or muscle testing as the means to find answers are surprisingly accurate and effective.

As the physical body changes from water-based to a light-based crystalline lightbody (already coded within us), our physical bodies will be radically different. However, at this stage of the transformation, we often experience various physical, emotional and mental ascension 'growing pains' - symptoms like headaches, back pain, flu-like symptoms, depression, etc. Also, any parts of the body that still hold blocked emotions will eventually show a problem on the physical level.

We already have our original perfect body blueprint imprinted within us, free of all the imperfections that we have picked up throughout our many life and death experiences. In order to reestablish that blueprint we must now make time to heal our bodies and allow the lightbody to come through. To do this, we need to pay attention to three things:

1) Our blueprint needs to be upgraded through the use of intention, the power of the mind which gives strong direction.

2) Our physical body needs a healthy routine to revitalize and sustain our new blueprint by getting enough rest, proper nutrients and exercise each day.

3) All emotional blocks need to be cleared to allow the transition to occur smoothly.

The Spiritual Scheme of Things

The picture on this page - representing one incarnated being and its spirit helpers in relationship to the Divine Body - presents my version of our interaction with the spirit realm. Each soul in the group is part of the Divine Body (the One, the Godhead, Source, etc.) and has its own group of soul helpers. Additionally the picture shows a couple ghosts, *discarnates* and a *separate* (a vigilante-type spirit) that are hanging around.

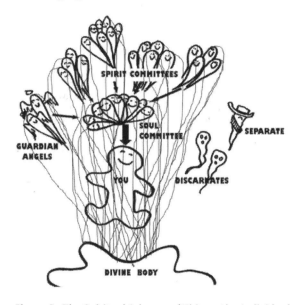

Figure 3   The Spiritual Scheme of Things: the Individual

Until very recently, most souls were engaged in multiple, concurrent incarnations in various dimensions, planets, galaxies, etc. Imagine this picture repeated eight times or more for one soul incarnated in eight different concurrent lifetimes and multiple times for each spirit helper involved in the various lifetimes. We work with each other in a variety of jobs on both the spiritual and physical planes connected by threads of energy, creating one giant matrix. Even though we seem to be separate individuals, we are constantly affecting one another and are ultimately part of the One.

In essence it is you and a group of spirit helpers who channel information when you use your pendulum, write a book, perform surgery, or do creative tasks. You do not work alone.

The following diagrams demonstrate how your soul's energy can be affected by the energy of its spirit helpers and why that must be taken into account during treatment and/or clearing work.

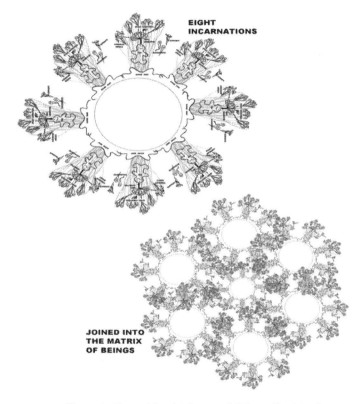

Figure 4   The Spiritual Scheme of Things: The Matrix

Beliefs Underlying the LifeWeaving System

- **You are a collection of vibrational bodies in a vibrational world**. Because of these various vibration levels, your body often holds engrams - memories of past traumatic events held in the neural tissue that will affect you lifetime after lifetime until the lessons are learned and cleared. For the LifeWeaving work, I have chosen to use one of the oldest and simplest explanations (of many differing existing theories) of the body levels and present them here:

o Physical body with its Etheric pattern.

o Astral - the energy body.

o Lower Mental-Causal, Buddhic and Atman - the three emotional bodies.

o Monad - the thought or mental body.

o Spiritual body - includes the soul twin, flame family, soul family and Source.

- **As a vibrational being, you are working with, and affected by, spirits around you,** including:

o **Your Soul or High Self Committee** - an elite group of high-level souls acting like a gentle but vigilant 'soul nanny,' looking out for a person's highest and best good. This is your spiritual self, the higher self.

o **Ascended Masters, Archangels** - high level spirits working directly with God.

o **Assigned Spirit Helpers** - the God-sanctioned guardian angels, guides and galactic guides working with a person.

o **Other Spirits** - These include two types of *discarnates*: (1) *ghosts*, souls who have died but haven't crossed over yet or are trapped by circumstances on the Earth plane, and (2) *separates*, souls who have crossed over but come back on their own accord with their own agenda. *Separates* mostly hinder since they do not work through a person's Soul Committee. *Separates*, with a higher vibrational rate than *ghosts*, are also more difficult to detect and often purposely hide themselves. Note that any spirit can hold "light" or "dark" energy, or even carry both.

- **We are affected by other spirits**. We can be affected by our spirit helpers as well as other spirits. If you have a specific physi-cal problem or addiction, you will often attract spirits who also vibrate to that issue, which in turn makes you more sensitive to the problem or addiction. The more you resonate to that specific energy, the worse you will feel. Also if you happen to be incarnated in a parallel universe where you are being tortured or dying, the energetic connection with that other self can 'blast open' into a concurrent life and negatively affect you.

- **We are members of a large soul group.**
  o **Soul family** - a group of many spirits working together on a particular project for Source.
  o **Flame family** - a group of 18 souls within the same soul family, working very closely together throughout various incarnations, offering support or helping each other clear karmic programs and learn lessons. During this process, flame family members also tend to create karmic issues with each other that eventually need to be cleared. The members of your flame family are all considered to be your soul mates while one is the exact other half of your original soul split.

Figure 5 The Soul Family Flower

- **As a spirit, you are unlimited.** Multi-dimensional theory states that "there are many levels of consciousness and that each level inhabits life energies, separate and unconscious of each other. Each exists in the same spot but vibrates at different `rates of speed." Therefore you can exist in this world at the same time that you exist as an incarnated being in some other world, dimension, or universe, or you can be a spiritual being acting as someone else's guardian angel, guide, or even as the guardian of a planet.

- **Reincarnation.** A person's life force does not cease to exist when the physical body dies but continues to exist as the soul-mind until he or she is reborn. This soul-mind requires many incarnations of emotional and intellectual experiences to help move it to perfection.

- **Past life experiences can affect us in other lifetimes.** As an individual, if we die while suppressing feelings of resentment, anger, fear or hatred for a person or a situation, those energies will be carried over into other lifetimes. These suppressed feelings then bring unwanted and unpleasant behavioral patterns or physical illness in later lifetimes until the charge of the original experience is released.

- **As above, so below.** Consider that the spirit realm may be as "messed up" as our own world because we are mirroring that state of affairs on a smaller scale. Hence before beginning a LifeWeaving session, all spirit helpers should be cleared.

- **Life is a play.** As you go through life consider that you and the other flame family members are researching some information for your soul family that is, in turn, researching a topic for Source. In order to thoroughly understand that topic, your flame family receives a "play script" to help with the research. Over many lifetimes your flame group performs that play again and again, taking new roles each lifetime. Eventually everyone involved experiences and gains an understanding of every single role and, as a result, the topic. Mission accomplished!

- **Everything is just the way it is**. All events have neutral energy and it is the observer who labels it as 'good' or 'bad'. Why do 'bad' things happen to us if this statement is true? Actually those 'bad' experiences can help us identify karmic programming that needs to be cleared or can move us into position for another lesson. Those experiences offer opportunities of what an incarnated period should provide: to learn, to grow and to keep moving   forward as spirits. Those souls who "hurt us" have often volunteered to wear the black hats and take on the role of "bad guy" - often a difficult role for them. Another lifetime you may be called upon to play a similar role for them.

- **Life is a mirror**. We are constantly being given reminders of things that need our attention through experiences or through interactions with other people. For example, if everyone around us shows anger, it is usually due to our own internal anger projecting outward.

Emotions—The Key to Healing

LifeWeaving evolved to help deal with emotional blocks. As an acupuncturist, I occasionally saw clients returning months later, after they had healed, with what seemed to be the same presenting problem. Obviously healing had not happened at some level. My diagnostic pendulum research into why this occurred always led to a cause of "emotional issues."

As a health care practitioner, I could not imagine everyone needing to spend years with psychiatrists, counselors or psychologists in order to heal emotions. This prompted me to study methods of rapid testing and clearing that worked on an emotional level. These included Spiritual Response Therapy (SRT), Neuro-Emotional Testing (NET), Quantum Touch, Kinesiology and Soul Retrieval. I integrated portions of many of these methods into the LifeWeaving charts and testing so that my method would be faster and, hopefully, more effective.

Recurring health issues, problems not healing, or even being prone to having a lot of accidents can be seen as signals being sent by the body to alert you to the existence of a deep blockage. I like to think of these signals as "cosmic 2x4's" used by spirit to get our attention.

Those signals or symptoms usually alert us to the presence of an emotional charge locked into our cells, organs or systems of the body by a traumatic occurrence from sometime in the past. This emotional charge stopped the flow of blood, energy and/or fluids to the area making it susceptible to pain and disease. The body retains a pattern for these signals and that pattern can be carried over from lifetime-to-lifetime. Therefore these emotional blocks need to be released before healing can fully take place or there is a high risk that the same or a similar form of health issue will recur at a later time.

For example, if a child breaks a wrist, the break leaves a physical scar which will heal. But a typical hospital treatment includes strange people, strange smells, needles, having the wrist painfully re-set, etc. All or part of that experience leaves a dormant emotional scar in the surrounding wrist tissue. Thirty years later, the (now) adult may walk into a dining room or bar, smell alcohol (associating with the hospital disinfectant) and at the same time see someone wearing a white sports jacket (associating with the white coats of the medical personnel). At that moment this sensory combination, generalized from the original hospital experience, awakens those cellular scar memories in the wrist which, in turn, trigger pain. Usually, the person never connects that pain to the childhood incident. All he or she knows is the sudden appearance of arm or wrist pain.

By clearing these hidden blocks, the presenting symptoms and overall emotional health of a person often shows amazing improvement. If the emotional block is not cleared or resolved

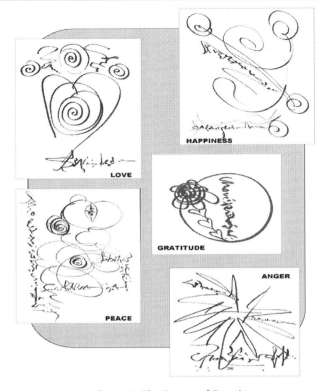

Figure 6 The Energy of Emotions

even if the blocked areas are surgically removed, a body will go back to the drawing board and begin to create a new signal to get one's attention. It might take a few years, but that underlying issue will find a way to return in some new form until the person finally listens to the message and resolves it! You must find and clear the cause - why you needed a signal in the first place - in order to heal completely!

Past Lives and Emotional Blocks

Very often these emotional scars are from past life experiences. Whatever emotions we were feeling at the time of an intense trauma or death locks into us and is stored on the astral body level. In a later life, those scars download with the new body pattern, eventually reaching the physical level and causing troublesome symptoms. For example, if you were hanged while feeling fearful or angry about the experience, those emotions of fear or anger settle into the neck area at the time of death. In a later lifetime, you may feel neck pain when you respond to a stressful situation involving anger or fear. Or if you were killed by a lion in a past life, in this life a house cat might cause an overwhelming and seemingly unreasonable fear or allergic response. Allergies can even be an attempt by your guardian angels to keep you away from some type of perceived danger similar to something that ended a previous life.

I have personally experienced how strong the physical reaction can be due to these cellular memories. One evening I was multi-tasking: working on my computer, cat in my lap, and half watching a TV program where contestants were vying for their own nature show. The format was patterned somewhat after the TV show *Survivor* but with a biology focus. This night each contestant, in turn, entered a jungle enclosure to first spot a six month-old tiger cub, then turn to the camera and talk about tigers, conservation efforts, and such. Two contestants in a row located the cub and then turned their backs on it to face the camera and, each time, the cub went into a 'playful' cat attack mode and charged! The cub's charge was broken at the last moment by a trainer whose job was to see that neither the animal nor any human was injured. After watching this with some amusement, I turned my attention back to my computer.

Figure 7   Tiger, Tiger!

A moment later, I glanced up and saw the third contestant back-peddling around a tree with his hands on the forehead of the cub, trying to keep it at bay. Upon seeing this, I experienced an immediate, intense stabbing pain in my right eye and that side of my face swelled up within seconds (as the cat in my lap went flying!). I used LifeWeaving to research and clear this painful issue immediately, but it was still almost a week before all the swelling went down and the last of the eye pain cleared.

The research confirmed that one of my lifetimes had ended with my head in the mouth of a tiger. My cells still retained memory of the event, reacting strongly upon seeing that particular scene on the television. Buried memories were triggered and brought up to my lower conscious mind, leading to the physical cellular reaction.

Months later I deliberately watched a re-run of the same episode without any visceral effects - it was simply an amusing scene - so I know I had successfully released all the cellular memory surrounding that incident with the LifeWeaving clearing.

Figure 8   Just a Cub

CHAPTER 3

Clearing and Protection

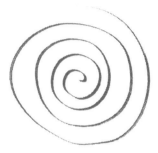

Figure 9   Clearing Symbol

What is Clearing?

According to the *Donning International Encyclopedic Psychic Dictionary*, *clearing* means "to release, flush out, or break up complexes in the subconscious mind so they do not cause problems in one's personality, life-style, or physical body." *Complexes* are feelings of guilt, hate, anxiety, resentment, jealousy, or the clinging to old theories, standards, and life-styles. These feelings, caused by the emotional pain of an event or by the restraint of today's culture, often times result in unpleasant and unwanted emotions being repeatedly repressed. Further, these repressed emotions grow and fester until they are forced to the surface and are put into their proper perspective. The action of clearing takes the energetic charge out of unpleasant events so they dissipate and never return.

Signs That You Need to Clear

- **Empathic Reactions**. If you start experiencing emotions such as anger or frustration and you don't normally react that way, you may be so energetically open or empathic that you are picking up everyone else's stuff.

- **Extreme and Unusual Emotions**. If you want to kick the cat or punch a hole in the wall, you probably have angry entities around you and are sharing their emotions even as they feed off of your reactions.

- **Everyone Else has a Problem**. When everyone around you seems angry and stressed they may be reacting to and mirroring your energy.

- **Everything is Going Wrong**. When everything in your life seems to be going wrong, realize that something IS wrong.

What You Should Clear

- **Your Own Stuff**. What is coming up for you personally.

- **Other's Stuff**. What you pick up from those around you due to empathy or increased sensitivity.

- **Contracts and Vows**. Any past-life contracts you have made to help others need to be revoked. Right now, each soul must take responsibility for itself and trying to clear programs for other souls doesn't ultimately help anyone.

- **Spirit Helpers' Stuff**. Our spirit helpers usually carry their own issues (*e.g.,* memories of addictions) that still need to be cleared. When such spirits connect to an incarnated being with similar problems, the intensity of those issues increases for the incarnated person.

Figure 10 What to Clear

Safeguards When Working with the Spirit World

When doing LifeWeaving clearing, we often have entities or spirits around us that need to be either cleared or removed.

The word *spirit* has the basic theme of "indestructible life" - the essence of the individual that never dies - like a guide, ghost, Earthbound entity, etc. Some spirits hold light energy while others are considered dark. Note that as you LifeWeave, you do not have to deal directly with any of these spirits. Instead call upon Archangel Michael and his team of helpers to intercede by removing unwanted entities from your presence.

An important consideration when dealing with spirits as well as other people's energy is to stay neutral without resistance. The more attention you place on a particular situation, the more you send out an energetic vibrational match to it and keep bumping into it. This is called the *Law of Attraction*.

 If you have a great deal of fear about working with spirits, that fear attracts them. Instead, laughter is best because the vibrational energy of laughter weakens that attraction.

Harry Potter and his classmates learned to deal with fear by working with a *boggart*, a spirit that took the form of what each of them feared most. They learned to cast the "Riddikulus Spell," changing the boggart from what they feared into something comical, thus completely draining its power over them and releasing any fear it had created.

Learn to laugh at your fears and let Archangel Michael's team do all the work!

Figure 11 The Keys to Safe Working

Protection Methods

- **Physical Level Protection.** Strengthen your protective energy field (what the Chinese call the *Wei Qi*) by utilizing the Violet Flame of Transmutation to keep it clear. Channeled by St. Germaine, this seventh ray of White Light helps (1) free us of negative forces or karmic influences; (2) connects us to Source and (3) transforms negative thoughts.

  You can also do a visualization exercise daily to strengthen your protective energy field:

  1) *Create a bubble of energy around you*
  2) *Now bring a white ball of light into the bubble above your head*
  3) *Begin compressing it with imaginary hands until it gets brighter and brighter, even as bright as the sun*
  4) *Finally burst the ball of light and let the White Light completely fill the bubble around you, fully strengthening your aura.*

- **Deflect Incoming Energy.** Surround yourself with objects like crystals, stones, crosses; use aromatherapy or essential oils like sage or Thieve's Oil or White Angelica (available from Young

Living); wear a special piece of clothing like a vest; use strengthening colors (use your favorite intuitive method to pick out power colors for yourself). Protective objects can be made by projecting mental energy onto the article and consecrating it for the primary purpose of protecting its owner from negativity.

- **Avoid Blocking!** The more power you throw at an opponent, the more force that opponent sends back to you. The more you fear something, the more power you give to it. Think of placing a gentle shield (like a spinning column of White Light) around you - enough to deflect and to change the direction of what is coming at you, allowing it to flow around you without any resistance.

- **Mental Level Protection.** Use clearing statements or call in helpers from the spiritual realm - especially Archangel Michael and his destroyer force angels. Also, saying the words *"Blood of Christ"* is highly protective.

- **Identify It - Don't Identify With It!** Remember to IDENTIFY what is affecting you, but DON'T IDENTIFY WITH IT! Simply let it pass through you and ground into the Earth without becoming mentally and emotionally invested in all its aspects. Just let it pass through and out. It just is.

CHAPTER 4

Important Dowsing Details for Practitioners

Critical Dowsing Differences When LifeWeaving

Several aspects of LifeWeaving dowsing are different than the general pendulum and chart techniques found in the literature. Below are some extremely important dowsing tips that will help ensure accuracy while you work with these charts.

- **Harmonize the *Personal Trinity* - The Self, Soul and Ego**

  Rather than filtering answers through a person's Higher Self as is the practice in regular dowsing, in LifeWeaving the *Invocation* is used to first harmonize the client's *Personal Trinity*: his/her Ego, Self and Soul Committee (Higher Self), and then to align this trinity with the Divine Plan, the universal program we are all part of (much like being one organ in the body). By working with all parts of the *Personal Trinity* we can receive input from our most wounded part - the Ego, and our strong-willed Self that is in charge of decision-making. Here are the parts of the *Personal Trinity*:

  o **The Ego** strongly influences the physical body - especially the three lower chakras - by responding primarily to fears and memories in matters of safety for the physical body, often using pain or emotions to get our attention.

○ **The Human Self**, which operates out of the heart chakra, sits between Ego and Soul and receives information to be considered and potentially acted upon. The Human Self has a large influence on health due to its use of free will and conscious decision making.

○ **The Higher Self** is concerned with spiritual development and relates more to the three upper chakras.

Figure 12 The *Personal Trinity*

Before beginning a dowsing session bring the *Personal Trinity* into *"perfect harmony, cooperation and agreement and aligned with the Divine Plan"* by reciting the *Invocation* found on the Power Chart.

Alternately, a practitioner can use the following method to harmonize the Personal Trinity:

1. Test the percentage that the Self and Soul are in harmony. If not at 100%, use the **LifeWeaving** process to find and clear all reasons and then bring them into 100% alignment.

2. Test what percentage the Ego is in harmony with this (now) aligned Self/Soul. Research and clear to 100%.

3. Ask to align this harmonized *Trinity* to the Divine Plan and make sure it is at 100%.

- **Each Dowsing Sequence Begins on a Neutral Line.** Always start your testing by placing your pendulum into a gentle neutral swing over the red neutral line on a *Chart Key* or Chart Section, then, with intention, add in the client and the issue to be cleared.

- **Allow for Multiple Answers.** As you test a section always allow for your pendulum to find more than one word at a time (if there are any).

- **Each Dowsing Sequence Ends on the Neutral Line** 'Train' your pendulum to return to the neutral line of the section you are testing after it finds all necessary *Keywords.* This confirms that your pendulum is finished with that section or chart.

- **When Dowsing a Section is Complete, Return to the Chart Key.** When your pendulum returns to and remains on neutral for a specific section, go back to the *Chart Key* neutral line to find your next action: to dowse another section on that chart, to switch to another chart, or to take your findings to the *Clearing Macro*. (Note that occasionally you may be sent back to the same section right away.)

- **Create an Imaginary Basket to Hold Answers Until Ready to Clear.** As you find the *Keywords* necessary to clear a blockage, have the client place them in an imaginary basket above his/her head until all are found for that particular topic. Once the *Keywords* with their associated energetic vibration are in the basket, spirit remembers them so you and the client do not have to. When your pendulum indicates *Clearing Macro* on the *Chart Key*, have the client envision "*Spiraling those words down through the mind, body and spirit...*". The complete *Clearing Macro* is found on the RESEARCH CHART or on page 65 of this manual.

- **Recognize that a New Layer is Ready to Clear.** As you say the *Clearing Macro*, allow your pendulum to move in a gentle neutral swing along the neutral line. If the pendulum drops off the line to the left of neutral, it indicates that another layer is ready to come up for research and clearing. If this happens, place the same issue you have been working on onto the neutral line and repeat the **LifeWeaving** process for the client.

Note: A drop to the right of neutral means that the client's assigned spirit helpers have the problem and need to be cleared. In that case say: "*Educate, elevate, remove or replace,*" and then retest that the problem has cleared. (See also pages 31-32)

- **Test Variations on the Original Issue.** Once a statement or issue tests neutral for the client, you should also try testing different but similar aspects of the problem. For example, after testing the word 'diabetes,' you can try 'high blood sugar,' 'glucose,' 'insulin resistance,' 'sugar problems,' etc. clearing any positives (where your pendulum moves off the neutral line) using the *Basic LifeWeaving Protocol*.

- **Do a Final *Completion Check* After Clearing.** As part of the *Completion Check*, test each part of the *Personal Trinity* (*i.e.*, Ego, Self, Soul) separately as occasionally one may only be a little out of balance and its signal is overwhelmed by the other (stronger) responses. Finally test the client's assigned spirit guides and guardian angels and other spirits as well for neutrality/completion. See page 65 for the *Completion Check*.

Other Dowsing Tips

- **Testing for the Source of Information**

During LifeWeaving dowsing, the goal is to be receiving answers through the harmonized *Personal Trinity* aligned with the Divine Plan/God.

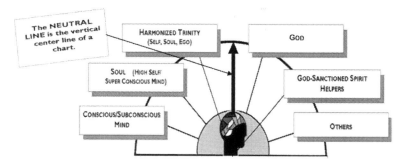

Figure 13 Information Sources Chart

Protocol to Test the Source of Received Information

1. Start with your pendulum in a neutral swing over the neutral line (the vertical line on the chart) and ask *'Who is giving me information?"* Always be open to the possibility of more than one answer.

2. Next ask *"Anyone else?"* This helps to avoid input from guides, separates, or other unwanted and untrustworthy sources.

Use the Information Sources sections as often as needed during a dowsing session to establish the quality of your answers.

If you are having difficulty, stop and ask your spiritual workers for clearing, remove any earthly distractions, and then say *"Connect me to my harmonized Soul Committee, High Self, Trinity and the Divine Plan at this time. "Am I 100% connected?"* Double-check again using the chart and then begin dowsing again if everything is clear and correct.

If any questionable answers arise, move off the chart and ask: *"Am I only getting information through my Harmonized Trinity and God?"* If *"yes,"* you are fine. If *"no,"* clear and recheck.

- **Where Dowsing Answers Can Come From**

The source of any answers obtained while dowsing determines how accurate your answers will be so it is critical to know how to check. Pendulum information can come from any or combination of the following sources:

- ○ **Conscious/Subconscious Mind**: the conscious mind is where we receive information from our five senses. This information is then manipulated to form judgments, reactions, emotions, and attitudes. The subconscious mind records and holds in memory all input from our consciousness; and the input becomes instincts and beliefs that will continue to act as filters throughout our lives. The conscious or subconscious mind is a very poor source of information!

- ○ **Soul or Superconscious Mind (High Self):** consists of an energy field that brings knowledge and information from a higher source that bypasses the conscious/subconscious mind. The superconscious mind is often referred to as oversoul, super ego, or High Self. It is often thought of as a collection or committee of spiritual entities that is charged with looking out for a soul's highest and best good throughout its existence, like a spiritual nanny.

- ○ **Harmonized *Personal Trinity***: consists of the Self, Soul and Ego being 100% in harmony. It allows the dowser to connect with not only the spiritual higher self but with the human self and the child-like ego which all hold keys to clearing the physical body. This level needs to be connected to the Divine Plan for highest accuracy.

- ○ **God/Source/Divine Plan**: consists of the overall order of everything in the universe where we function. Accurate information comes from this level and is used in combination with the harmonized *Personal Trinity.*

o **God-Sanctioned Spirit Helpers**: consist of spirits working with you (like a guardian angel) that have been "approved" by Source. This information is very unreliable as these spirits might wish to shield you from a certain piece of information, or try to add their own point of view (like a dark energy or unclear spirit working with you as a guide). If this source is suspected, stop and reaffirm that you are working only through the Trinity-God connection. Demand it!

o **Others:** consist of other entities or beings (spirits or in the flesh) hanging around you - not officially part of your God-sanctioned "team." They have no vested interest in complete and honest answers nor do they care about your highest and best good. *Others* usually attach to you for reasons of their own. A skeptical friend or spouse can also influence answers, especially if you are just learning to dowse.

▪ **Utilizing the Neutral Line for Testing.** A good way to speed up dowsing work is by using the neutral line on any chart as a baseline. To dowse how something will affect a particular person, place your pendulum into a gentle swing along the neutral line and, either mentally or verbally, add in the person and whatever needs to be tested. Observe what happens to the pendulum swing.

Results can be interpreted as follows:

o If the pendulum remains in a neutral swing, there is no problem or disharmony with what is being tested.

o If the pendulum moves to the left of the neutral line, the client has an imbalance that needs to be researched and cleared. The degree the pendulum moves gives an approximation of how much disharmony exists.

o If instead, the pendulum moves to the right of the neutral line, there is an imbalance for the client's spirit helper or helpers and they should be cleared. Say *"Educate, elevate, remove or replace as needed."*

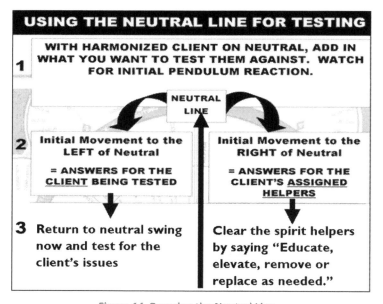

Figure 14 Dowsing the Neutral Line

By using this method, a dowser can test many things in a short period of time. This can be especially helpful when allergy testing. For example, if someone shows an imbalance to milk, this imbalance can be tested further placing by mentally placing the person being tested on the neutral line, and then individually adding in specific types of milk such as cow, soy, rice, coconut, goat, whole, 2%, non-fat, etc. In a matter of seconds, exactly what type of milk he or she is allergic or sensitive to and a rough estimate of the intensity of the allergy can be determined and then cleared or acted upon. In the above example, he/she might be allergic to soy, whole and non-fat cow's milk, but okay (neutral) with 2% cow's milk.

After using **LifeWeaving** to clear an allergy, recheck the person by adding them to the neutral line along with variations of what they are sensitive to, imposed mentally one by one onto the neutral line. The pendulum should remain in a neutral swing over the line.

Note that if an allergy is life threatening, as with shellfish or peanuts, warn your client to be careful if consuming or exposing him or herself to that specific allergen. Many allergies are complex and there may be more layers that need clearing to make the substance totally safe.

- **Working with Complex Charts.** As you work with a complex dowsing chart that includes several layers of information, focus on the information section that you need and ignore the remainder.

- **Multiple Practitioners Researching the Same Subject.** Multiple practitioners will often obtain different answers when clearing the same question. The primary reason is that each dowser has his or her own belief systems, knowledge levels, and interests that act as filters. These answers are not wrong, but are typically different aspects of an issue.

  A second reason for finding different answers is that a dowser may have had a part or role in the experience being cleared. If this happens, answers are found that will help with his or her own clearing. For example, if you are clearing a past-life experience between two people, your own guardian angel may bring you in as a third character in order to clear the interaction that you had experienced in that lifetime with those souls.

- **Magnifying Readouts.** As you work with the charts, if you are ever unsure whether or not the pendulum has moved just slightly off neutral, say *"Magnify the chart"* and recheck. Magnifying instantly recalibrates your 10–100% scale down to 1–10%, allowing you to easily distinguish a very slight imbalance that may still exist.

- **Clarifying Results**. If unsure which chart item is being indicated by your pendulum, mentally take the two words off the chart and test again for *"This one or that one?"*

CHAPTER 5

LifeWeaving Tools

LifeWeaving System Upgrades

As we progress from the 3rd to the 5th dimensions, the LifeWeaving clearing system (used in some form for over 15 years) was in need of a makeover. Through the addition of *Chart Keys*, a dowser can easily integrate all three system charts by automatically being directed to specific sections of a chart for data gathering. The *Chart Keys* also give an indication when to switch to a different chart, and/or when to apply the *Clearing Macro*.

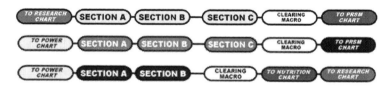

Figure 15   Chart Keys

The other changes include a few tweaks to chart content, changes to the *Basic LifeWeaving Protocol*, and the introduction of new protocols. In order to update testing and clearing, the archetypes and blocks sections have been swapped between earlier versions of the POWER and RESEARCH charts. The PRSM DIAGNOSIS chart, last revised in August 2014, has only slightly changed. The *Invocation* was added to the POWER CHART to streamline the preliminary work and help ensure that the client is clear and answers will be accurate.

LifeWeaving Charts and Manuals

The **LifeWeaving** charts and manuals have been revised and simplified over the years of use. The manuals, which describe in detail each element mentioned in the various chart sections, have been combined into one reference guide for the three main charts.

The **LifeWeaving** charts can be used independently of each other or together as a system. Before you begin a session, set your intention to use 1, 2 or all three charts and instruct spirit to stick with the options you lay out. For example, say "*I am only using the* POWER LIFEWEAVING CHART *and want all answers necessary for healing to originate from there!*"

POWER CHART Components

The POWER CHART is the basic dowsing chart used with the **LifeWeaving** clearing system and is always the first chart to begin with. The chart includes these major items:

- The *Invocation*: Used to clear and prepare the client for a session using White Light, the Violet Flame and your *I AM* presence to clear and align the *Personal Trinity*, soul committee, guides and guardian angels and to harmonize all to the Divine Plan.

- Section A: Used to determine *Colors, Life Areas, Elements, Who to Call Upon for Help, Chakras, Activities, Affirmations* and *Responsibilities.*

- Section B: Used to determine *Source of Dowsed Information, Three Kingdoms* (Angelic, Human and Elemental), *Time, Body Levels, Mayan Scale of Consciousness,* and *Body Categories.*

- Section C: Used to determine what *Archetypes* are involved.

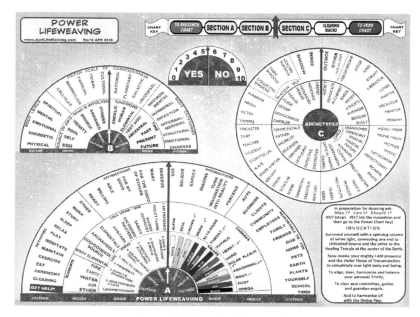

Figure 16 POWER LIFEWEAVING CHART

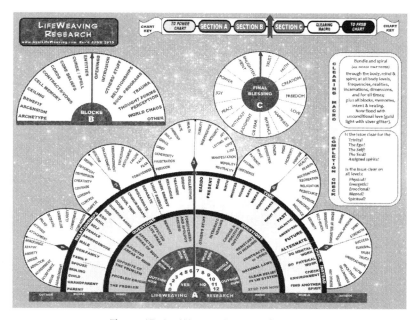

Figure 17 LIFEWEAVING RESEARCH CHART

- Yes/No and 0-10/0-100: Used to determine *Numbers, Percentages,* simple *Yes and No* answers.

RESEARCH CHART Components

- Section A Topics: Include *Questions, Relationships, Time, Check Instead,* and *the Keyword petals.*

- Section B Topic: Several different types of common *Blocks* are listed that may need further attention during a clearing session.

- Section C: Used as a source for necessary *Keywords,* as a *Final Blessing* to close a session, or to dowse for *Messages from Spirit.*

- Completion Check: Used to determine whether the **LifeWeaving** clearing has been successfully completed on all body levels and portions of the harmonized *Personal Trinity.*

- *Clearing Macro*: Used throughout the **LifeWeaving** clearing protocol to move healing energies through the body, mind and spirit to complete clearing.

PRSM DIAGNOSIS CHART Components

The PRSM CHART is used for diagnostic testing. The initials PRSM stand for "Pendulum Research Sourcing Method," originally a way to indicate diagnosis without actually using the term (stemming from the days when only medical doctors had the right to 'diagnose').

- Section A Key: Used before dowsing the Descriptors Chart in order to find the system to research and the number of the organ or meridian in that system. This key includes *Body Levels, Organ Systems, Numbers* and *Source of Pendulum Information.*

- Section A Descriptors: Used to determine any *Environmental, Hormonal, Infection, Internal/Meridial, Structural, Chakra* and *Emotional* factors that can affect health.

- **Section B Topics:** Deaths - Used to research *Past Life Deaths* (what, how and why) as needed to help determine why a client has certain health conditions or fears.

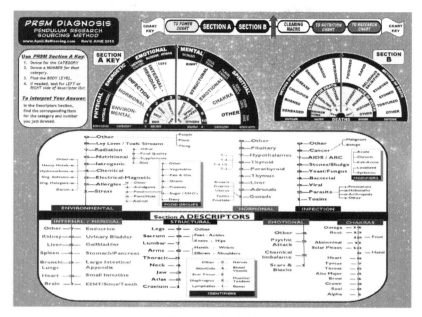

Figure 18 PRSM CHART

LifeWeaving Worksheet

A practitioner can have more confidence in the accuracy of a session by using the LifeWeaving Worksheet to check that the *Invocation* did what it was supposed to, to keep track of results and changes, as well as a way to remember and work with the information that comes up during a session.

Uses for the Worksheet
- The *Preparedness Checklist* of what should have been cleared by reading the *Invocation*.
- *Supplemental Questions* that you can test as needed for a case.
- To jot down some notes during your intake with the client. You can include what the main concern is, names of all the

'players' that will be part of a session, phrases that 'jump out' for further testing, etc.

- A place to jot down repeating phrases, issues, archetypes or ages that come up during a clearing so you can return later and test them individually with LifeWeaving and see if there is more to clear around them or to include on a report for a long distance client.

- As a reference for previous sessions to identify changes and note progress.

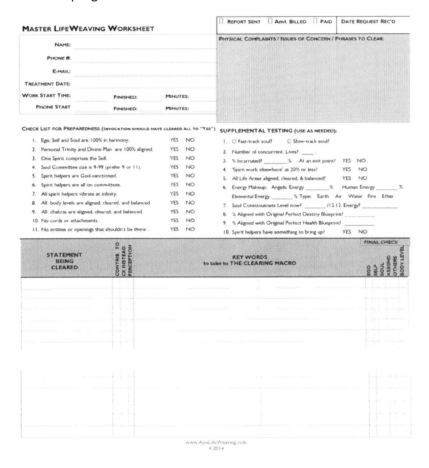

Figure 19   LifeWeaving Worksheet

*(A free 8 1/2 x 11 download of the 2-sided worksheet
is available at www.AyniLifeWeaving.com)*

Check List for Preparedness Questions

Used to insure that reciting the *Invocation* did prepare a client for a LifeWeaving session. All 11 questions should test as "*yes*" and any "*no*" answers need to be cleared before moving further into a session. The questions are as follows:

1.	Ego, Self and Soul are 100% in harmony.	YES	NO
2.	Personal Trinity and Divine Plan are 100% aligned.	YES	NO
3.	One Spirit comprises the Self.	YES	NO
4.	Soul Committee size is 9-99 (prefer 9 or 11).	YES	NO
5.	Spirit helpers are God-sanctioned.	YES	NO
6.	Spirit helpers are all on committees.	YES	NO
7.	All spirit helpers vibrate at infinity.	YES	NO
8.	All body levels are aligned, cleared, and balanced.	YES	NO
9.	All chakras are aligned, cleared, and balanced.	YES	NO
10.	No cords or attachments.	YES	NO
11.	No entities or openings that shouldn't be there .	YES	NO

If any of the above questions do test as "no," they must be cleared. The following section gives detailed instructions for clearing each item listed along with more information about what an answer means for the dowser:

1. "Ego, Self and Soul are 100% in harmony."

   To Test: Use any number chart to obtain a percentage.

   Target Result: The client's Ego, Self and Soul must test at 100% harmony before beginning work.

   To Clear:

   a) Using a number chart, ask '*What % harmony between the Self and Soul?*' as the issue to clear.

   b) If not at 100%, find all *Keywords* using **LifeWeaving**.

   c) Apply the *Clearing Macro* to clear all *Keywords* found.

d) Continue clearing until 100% harmony is achieved.

e) Now check "*What percent is the Ego in harmony with the now aligned Self-Soul?*"

f) Clear as needed until all three parts are 100% aligned.

2. *"Personal Trinity* and Divine Plan are 100% aligned"

To Test: Use any number chart to obtain a percentage.

Target Result: The *Personal Trinity* (Harmonized Ego/Self/Soul) must test at 100% alignment with the Divine Plan before beginning work.

To Clear: LifeWeave using *"% Harmony between the Trinity and Divine Plan?"* as the issue to clear:

a) Find all *Keywords* by using the *Basic LifeWeaving Protocol.*

b) Apply the *Clearing Macro* using all *Keywords* found.

c) Retest percentage that the *Trinity* and Divine Plan are in harmony.

d) Continue clearing until 100% is achieved.

3. "One Spirit Comprises the Self"

To Test: Use any number chart and test the number of digits, then ask to see the number.

Target Result: One.

To Clear (if more than one):

a) Destroy all vows and contracts made with other spirits and then retest.

b) If still two or more, LifeWeave POWER CHART *Sections A, B* and *C* to find all *Keywords* involved in holding these spirits to you; apply the *Clearing Macro* and then retest.

c) After completing Steps A and B in this section, if there are still two spirits comprising the Self, ask *"Is the second soul the Twin*

Soul?" If NO, go back to Steps A and B and try again. If the answer is still YES, work with both spirits. (See the discussion below.)

Discussion: More than one spirit comprising the Self suggests multiple spirits are inhabiting the body, much like a person having multiple personalities. These can usually be removed easily with **LifeWeaving** or often just with intention. Clear any *"curses, contracts, heart vows, hidden vows or soul programs"* between the entities and the client, demanding that the unwanted spirits clear out!

However, if you clear down to two spirits, and the second one refuses to leave, it may be the person's exact soul twin - the other half of the monadic split that occurred when we first started to incarnate. If this happens, clear both the client and the twin (both separately and together) during a session. Harmonize them as much as possible by clearing any standing programs between them by placing your pendulum on the neutral line of the POWER *Chart Key*, adding in the two souls, then asking to see *"What is going on between them?"* and clearing any *Keywords* that come up.

4. "Soul Committee size is 9-99"

To Test: Using any number chart; find the number of digits, then ask to see what the number is.

Target Result: The number should fall within the range of 9-99 and be an uneven number. Nine or eleven is preferred.

To Clear if the Soul Committee is greater than 99:

a) Destroy any contracts or vows the client has with any of these spirits.

b) Demand that they sort themselves out by saying *"Educate, elevate, remove or replace"* and that you only want *"the best and brightest, the highest level souls that are free of all blocks and programs to remain."*

c) LifeWeave as necessary to clear.

Discussion: A lower number is better (a small committee gets more work done), as is an uneven number (no tie votes). Often spirits will move onto a soul committee for the experience and are not at as high a level of soul consciousness as the person to which they attach. When that happens, it is like receiving information from a child who means well but doesn't have enough experience or knowledge to give complete and/or correct answers. Those need to be removed. Also note that "old souls" tend to attract a lot of extra helpers.

5. **"Spirit Helpers are all God-Sanctioned (approved by God)?"**

To Test: Use any YES-NO chart.

Target Result: YES.

To Clear:

a) Destroy any vows or contracts between yourself or your client and any non-sanctioned spirits.

b) Demand that the spirits *"Educate, elevate, remove or replace as needed"* then re-test. If the helpers are still NOT all God-sanctioned, continue to Step C below.

c) LifeWeave POWER CHART *Sections A, B* and *C* for any *Key-words* holding spirits to the client and apply the *Clearing Macro*; re-test. If the client is still not clear, proceed with caution as answers may be incorrect.

Discussion: We need to always work both consciously and subconsciously with guides and guardian angels that are sanctioned or approved by God and be aware if others have slipped in uninvited.

6. **"Spirit Helpers are all on committees"**

To Test: Use any YES-NO chart.

Target Result: YES.

To Clear:

a) Demand the spirits *"either move onto committees or be removed"*; then re-test.

b) If helpers are NOT all on committees, LifeWeave POWER CHART *Sections A, B* and *C* for *Keywords* holding them and apply the *Clearing Macro*; re-test. If still not clear, proceed but with caution as answers may be incorrect.

Discussion: When we have too many spirit helpers the lines of information (on what I like to call my "head-set") are not clear. It is like walking into an airport and shouting out *"Does anyone know what time it is?"* Hundreds of people may start shouting back various times or other information like "my watch is broken" in a jumble of answers and languages that ultimately don't make any sense. This scene is similar to having a confused jumble of spirit helpers surrounding you. Instead, picture the many spirit guide committees meeting in their individual boardrooms, discussing your query about time, then taking a vote on what answer to send to you. That one answer is passed to your Soul Committee that then decides if it is for your highest and best good to give you the message. If so, you get a very clear answer.

7. **"Spirit Helpers all vibrate at an infinite level"**

To Test: Use any YES-NO chart.

Target Result: YES.

To Clear if NO:

a) Demand the spirits *"Educate, elevate, remove or replace as needed, making them the best and brightest and highest level possible."* then re-test.

b) Consciously destroy any vows or contracts you might have concerning holding on or helping lower level spirits; then re-test.

c) If helpers are NOT all at a frequency above a 12.12 consciousness level - LifeWeave POWER CHART *Sections A, B* and *C* for any *Keywords* and apply the *Clearing Macro*; re-test. If still not clear, proceed but with caution as answers may be incorrect.

Discussion: An "old soul" - one who has incarnated a lot - often picks up lower level spirits because of past karmic programs and also because an old soul is fun to hang out with for many of the "younger" entities. The presence of these less experienced spirits is like having a group of children trying to help you with some technical project: the kids are enthusiastic but tend to get in the way due to their lack of expertise.

Note: If a person starts with helpers who are calibrating very low, you may not be able to clear them all the way to infinity during a session. However, recheck near the end of your **LifeWeaving** session and you may find that the situation has improved due to the other clearing work done.

8. **"Body levels are all aligned, cleared and balanced"**

To Test: Use any YES-NO chart.

Target Result: YES.

To Clear if "NO" tests:

a) Use the POWER CHART *Section B, Body Levels* to identify what level is out of alignment by placing your pendulum into a gentle swing along the neutral line of *Section B* and ask the question "*What level or levels are out of alignment?*" Allow the pendulum time to indicate more than one if needed.

b) LifeWeave POWER CHART *Sections A, B* and *C* and for any *Keywords*.

c) Apply the *Clearing Macro*; then re-test.

Discussion: Note that if a person has experienced a car accident or other traumatic situation, one or more body levels will often slightly pop out of alignment and must be realigned in order for any healing work to completely integrate throughout all the levels. Note also that if body levels are out of alignment, it is common to also find chakras out of alignment. If so, ask if clearing work can be done for both at the same time.

Ways to Align the Body Levels

- Clear using the *Basic LifeWeaving Protocol*; or

- Tell your client to "*Breathe deeply and visualize stuffing your energetic, emotional and mental bodies into the smaller physical form - much like stuffing a sleeping bag into its stuff sack. Once this is done, anchor all the bodies at the feet by mentally fastening them together.*" Afterwards, recheck that the alignment was successful. The various body levels will automatically return to their original size and all should be in alignment.

9. **"Chakras are all infinitely opened, aligned, cleared and balanced"**

   To Test: Use any YES-NO chart.

   Target Result: YES.

   To Clear if a "NO" is indicated:

   a) Use POWER CHART *Section A Chakras* (Alpha to Omega) to find the problem chakra(s).

   b) LifeWeave the POWER CHART *Sections A, B* and *C* for any *Keywords*; if directed, go to the RESEARCH CHART *Section A* for any *Keywords* causing mis-alignment or imbalance.

   c) Apply the *Clearing Macro* to all *Keywords* found; then re-test.

   Discussion: There are many other methods that will work to clear the chakras besides **LifeWeaving**, so choose whichever you prefer.

10. **"No cords or attachments"**

    To Test: Use any YES-NO chart.

Target Result: YES.

To Clear:

o **Cords** - bring in a spiritual team of surgeons to remove the cord or cords, including the roots, and then to heal the area. While the healing is being applied, "light" the released cord with forgiveness and unconditional love and let it "burn" like a fuse back to the soul that sent it.

o **Attachments** - Call back your spirit, letting go of worries and concerns and instead concentrate on staying in the present moment.

Discussion: Cords are conduits or lines, sent by someone else (close by, distant, over the phone, or even from a past life) that attach to a person and severely drain energy like a vampire drains blood. The person doing the cording may be aware of what is happening (and cording on purpose) but often is, instead, very needy and may not be conscious of the act. The person being corded usually experiences a sudden intense drop in energy - feeling fine one minute and barely able to keep eyes open the next.

A client with attachments is leaking his or her own energy by not staying in present time. For example, even before getting out of bed in the morning, this person begins to worry about what to fix for dinner, where will he or she park at work, hate for a former spouse, etc.

11. **"No entities or openings that shouldn't be there"**

   To Test: Use any YES-NO chart.

   Target Result: YES.

   To Clear:

   a) Destroy any contracts or vows between yourself (or the client) and the entities.

b) Have Archangel Michael's team close and seal all openings.

c) Call upon his team to "*Check identifications and remove any spirits that do not belong*"; then circle yourself or client with White Light and the Violet Flame.

d) Re-test until clear or stop work for the time being until you can get yourself clear.

Discussion: If there are a large number of dark entities, or they are found often, check for spirit gates or energetic openings at the home or business, and ask that *"Archangel Michael and his team close and seal the openings and remove the spirits who came through the gate."* Openings or spirit gates are common in areas of chaos or clutter, recreational drug use, or where there are ley lines or toxic streams.

Supplemental Testing (Use as needed)

1. □ Fast-track soul?   □ Slow-track soul?

2. Number of concurrent Lives? _____ .

3. % Incarnated? _____%   At an exit point?   YES   NO

4. 'Spirit work elsewhere' at 20% or less?   YES   NO

5. All Life Areas aligned, cleared, & balanced?   YES   NO

6. Energy Makeup: Angelic Energy _____%   Human Energy _____ %

Elemental Energy _____ % Type: Earth   Air   Water   Fire   Ether

7. Soul Consciousness Level now? _____ /12.12. Energy? _____

8. % Aligned with Original Perfect Destiny Blueprint? _____

9. % Aligned with Original Perfect Health Blueprint? _____

10. Spirit helpers have something to bring up?   YES   NO

Before beginning **LifeWeaving** clearing, the *Supplemental Testing* questions can help obtain a useful snapshot of your client's current health and energy standings, but these are not always needed each session.

The ten questions, their purpose and how to test for them follow:

1. "Is this soul fast track or slow track?"

To Test: Dowse the two options.

Target Result: None - for information only.

Discussion: A fast track soul does not incarnate often, working primarily as spirit through most 'lifetimes.' As a result, the fast tracker pre-programs a lot of drama and trauma into his or her life in order to keep clearing karmic and soul programs while in a physical form. A slow tracker incarnates often so they move and think slower, deliberate a lot more than a fast tracker, and can often get mired down during a life - but 'no problem' as they will reincarnate soon and try again. These two types can have problems with each other due to their "speed" differences in acting and reacting to life.

2. "What is the number of concurrent lives?"

   To Test: Use any number chart.

   Target Result: One life is preferred.

   To Clear:

   a) If one is tested, this step is complete.

   b) If more than one is tested: Visualize the threads of energy connecting the client to all his or her other incarnations and mentally place a filter on each connected thread. Then have the client take a couple deep breaths and let spirit pull him or her out of any other life, wherever appropriate (let spirit decide!), and bring the energy back and integrate it into this lifetime, filtered free of any issues or energies from those other lives.

   c) Retest how many lives are still ongoing concurrently.

   d) If a person cannot be pulled out of another life as their work is not done yet, simply place a filter on the thread connecting the lives to reduce "cross-contamination."

   Discussion: Being incarnated allows us to clear karmic programs from other lifetimes and, possibly, to create new karma during the current life. Ten years ago most of us were incarnated in many concurrent lives but due to the increasing frequencies with Earth moving through this latest ascension attempt, we are needing to concentrate on what is happening here and now, utilizing just one incarnation as most souls are.

3. "What % is the client incarnated?"

   To Test: Use any number chart to obtain a percentage.

   Target Result: No fixed target; this is for gathering information.

   To Clear: See the discussion.

   Discussion: If a client is very ill, this is a useful number to know by helping both to determine the severity of a problem as well as to obtain a baseline for their condition. As you work, you can track the changes.

   Also, if a person registers at a low percentage of incarnation, you can LifeWeave to "*Clear any karmic reasons they have for living,*" then "*Clear any reasons they have for dying.*" This removes karmic influences and leaves them at neutrality where free will takes over.

   "At an exit point?"

   To Test: Use any yes-no chart.

   Target Result: Information only.

   To Clear: See discussion.

   Discussion: Before we come into a life, we set up seven exit points that give us the opportunity to get out of a life if all work is done or things are too messed up to make it work. These exit points can involve an accident, surgery gone wrong, or some other mishap that allow us to die without committing suicide.

   If a client is at an exit point period, clear any karmic reasons for living, and any karmic reasons for dying. He or she can then use free will to decide what to do.

4. "Is the client's spirit work less than 20%?"

To Test: Use any YES-NO chart or use a number chart to obtain the percentage.

Target Result: YES, 20% or less.

To Clear: Ask the client to *"Call back your spirit and send in teams of angels in your place.*

Discussion: While we are incarnated, our infinite spirit can also be working in many places at the same time, acting as guide, guardian angel, spiritually helping at a disaster, or perhaps even as god of a planet in some other galaxy. However due to the intense impact of ascension changes here on planet Earth, our focus and energy is needed here. Note also that some persons will purposely leave energetically and spend a lot of time helping elsewhere as spirits. These people are the "mothers and givers" of the world or they may be very galactic who, on a subconscious level, don't really want to be on this planet.

5. **"Are all Life Areas Fully Aligned, Cleared and Balanced?"**

    To Test: Use any YES-NO chart.

    Target Result: YES.

    To Clear (if more than one Life Area is indicated, clear one at a time):

    a) Dowse the POWER CHART *Section A Life Areas* to find the problem area(s).

    b) *"What percent is the Life Area out of balance?"*

    c) LifeWeave POWER *Sections A, B* and *C* for any *Keywords* that are affecting the balance.

    d) Apply the *Clearing Macro* and re-check for the new percentage of balance on the Life Area you are clearing. Continue to LifeWeave until the area is at 100% balance.

    Discussion: The nine Life Areas are borrowed from *Feng Shui*, the Chinese Art of Placement.

6.   "% Galactic/Angelic Energy? ___% Human Energy? ___%
Elemental Energy (fire, earth, water, air, ether) _____%?"

To Test: Use any number chart to test for percentages.

Target Results: Information only.

To Clear: Information only so no need.

Discussion: Earth is one of the "library planets" in this universe meaning that we hold the DNA for any star race that ever existed. Humans are mostly hybrids, holding some human, elemental and/or alien DNA. As we move further into the ascension process, these percentages can change as more DNA activations occur. If a person is very galactic, with a high percentage of active alien DNA, he or she will often have trouble grounding themselves, and will often feel lonely - as though nowhere on this planet seems like home.

A person with a high amount of elemental energy is usually small with fine, fairy-like features.

7. **"Soul Consciousness Level at This Time? Energy?"**

To Test: Use any number chart. The possible range is 3.0 to 12.12 with each dimension having 12 octaves or levels.

a) Find the consciousness level of the client at the time of the session.

b) Add the client to the RESEARCH CHART neutral line plus the question *"What energy best describes them now?"*

Target Result: Information only.

To Clear: No clearing is needed.

Discussion: We are presently moving from the 3rd to the 5th dimension (the 4th being non-physical). By tracking with this scale, the practitioner can get clues as to what type of physical and emotional issues the client will most likely be experiencing. Note that you are testing the highest level possible at which the client's soul has reached. If he or she tests at 5.8 (5th dimension, 8th octave) it means that the client can function from lower 3rd dimension up to high 5th. This range can change somewhat from day to day depending on what the client does, reads, where he or she spends time, etc. For example, during meditation, he or she will be at the highest part of the range; if shopping for groceries or drinking in a bar, at the lower end.

Another use for this scale of consciousness is to test whether a client is at a high enough level to accept energetic healing work. People at the lower ranges tend to prefer hands on methods and shy away from the metaphysical.

8. "% Aligned with Original Perfect Destiny Blueprint?"

To Test: Use any number chart and check for percentage.

Target Result: 100%.

To Clear: See Chapter 8 page 75, Advanced Protocols.

Discussion: At the time we incarnate, we hold a complete blueprint within us of our original destiny path. However, often an incident takes place - especially during childhood - that side tracks us. By healing this incident, we can be moved closer to or back onto that original path.

9. "% Aligned with Original Perfect Health Blueprint?"

To Test: Use any number chart and check for percentage.

Target Result: 100%.

To Clear: See Chapter 8 page 75, Advanced Protocols.

Discussion: At the time we incarnate, we hold a complete blueprint within us of our original perfect body. However due to emotional blocks, accidents and disease, that blueprint becomes sullied. By clearing it with **LifeWeaving**, the client can move closer to, or back into, that original perfect blueprint.

10. Spirit Guides want to bring something up?

To Test: Use any YES-NO chart

Target Result: Information.

To Clear if YES:

a) Place your pendulum, the client, and "*What do the spirit guides want to bring up?*" on the neutral line of the POWER *Chart Key.*

b) Find all *Keywords* that apply to the message.

c) Send all *Keywords* through the *Clearing Macro* when indicated; infuse unconditional love. Retest for completeness.

d) Retest for "*Anything else the spirit guides want to bring up?*" LifeWeave normally until the pendulum indicates neutrality.

Discussion: This gives a person's spirit guides the chance to bring up something for clearing that is needed but that might not have been otherwise addressed.

CHAPTER 6

Preparing for a Session

The initial clearing and alignment of both the dowser and the client are extremely important. Dowsing often fails because of poor questions, a suspect source of information, interference from other spirits, or the practitioner not being clear.

However the practitioner chooses to prepare for a session, he or she should be sure to include the following tasks:

1. Clear your energy field by reading the *Invocation*, doing a pre-session meditation, or using your own preferred method.
2. Set up personal protections as desired.
3. Obtain permission to work.
4. Set up a healing grid around the client and a White Light tunnel between you two.
5. Read the *Invocation* to prepare the client.

Elements of Practitioner Preparation

White Light - The LifeWeaving *Invocation* prepares both practitioner and client for a session by using one of the prime ingredients for safe work - the use of White Light. White Light contains the energies of all elements and chemicals found in the sun; is the basis for all color, and is pure in its essence. White Light represents totality, the absolute, the Holy Trinity. White is pure love, perfect love is pure and perfect love is all, therefore White Light is ALL.

Figure 20   White Light Symbol

If you ever feel a quick need for protection, ask for a cone of White Light to drop down around you. The protection is instantaneous and will last approximately30 minutes.

Obtain Permission to Work - Always obtain permission to work on yourself and/or others by asking the Soul Committee/Higher Self *"May I? Can I? Should I?"* If any of these questions returns a "no" answer, try to remove the block by simply saying *"Clear if possible."* If you still get a "no" answer, stop working until permission can be obtained.

During a session you may also need to ask for permission to work on other souls (incarnated or spirit) that will be part of your session. These can be relatives or friends or even spirit guides, guardian angels or entities seeking clearing that are attracted by the dowsing work. Get permission to work on them and then apply a "turbo clear" - meaning that the preparatory clearing is automatically done without the need to personally go through the process step by step. Be sure to check further if you feel it is needed.

Set Up Clearing Committees for Assistance - Use intention to set up pendulum clearing committees on the etheric realm to work with any spirits who either might try to drop in or who must be asked to leave during a session. This way you can always stay focused on the client's line of inquiry.

At any time during a session, feel free to call upon Archangel Michael and his team to clear you or the area you are in or just to lend support to the clearing process.

Figure 21 Archangel Michael

Pre-Session Meditation--can be recited to prepare for a session or you can use the *Invocation* found on the POWER CHART.

Take a deep breath.

Visualize yourself in a tall column of White Light, running from Unlimited Source above to the Crystalline Healing Temple at the Center of the Planet below you.

With your mind, start the column of White Light spinning (in either direction), moving it faster and faster until it is a white blur. Feel the spinning White Light clear your energy fields, open your chakras and circuits, and increase your frequency.

Take a deep, full integrating breath.

Call in your I AM presence, the individualized Presence of God within you.

Bring in the Violet Flame of Transmutation and Unconditional Love into your heart.

Take a deep integrating breath.

Now call in Archangel Michael and the Angels of Blue Flame to surround you on all sides, above and below; request that they remove all discarnates, separates, or dark energy beings; close any openings and remove any intruders. Ask these angels to enfold and protect you throughout the session.

Take a deep integrating breath.

Center yourself, move into a place of total neutrality, and ask "May I? Can I? Should I begin my work?"

Affirm "I AM aligned, sealed and protected in the Light and prepared to dowse."

Elements of Patient Preparation

The *Invocation*

In preparation for dowsing ask:
May I? Can I? Should I?
NO? (stop). YES? (do the invocation and then go to the Power Chart Key)

INVOCATION

Surround yourself with a spinning column of white light, connecting one end to Unlimited Source and the other to the Healing Temple at the center of the Earth.

Now invoke your mighty *I AM* presence and the Violet Flame of Transmutation to completely over light body and being,

To align, clear, harmonize and balance the personal Trinity,

To clear soul committee, guides and guardian angels,

And to harmonize *all* with the Divine Plan.

Note that if you are doing **LifeWeaving** clearing on someone else, just change the words of the *Invocation* (I, my, etc.) to fit the situation (you, your, etc.). Also be sure to obtain permission (*May I? Can I? Should I?*) to work on that person before starting the *Invocation*.

How the *Invocation* Works

- Spinning a column of White Light around you protects by reversing the infiltration of worldly thoughts and feelings in and around you. Connecting the column to Source gives you unlimited strength and to Earth gives you continual grounding.

- The *Invocation* invokes your mighty *I AM* presence and the Violet Flame. The *I AM* Presence is the divine spark of Totality in all humans; a sacred connection with one's true self; the Christ within. The Violet Flame of Transmutation transforms unwanted conditions and energies, and balances all by its Light.

- The *Invocation* harmonizes the *Personal Trinity* - the Ego, Self, and Soul - to prepare the client so the practitioner can achieve the best answers since all three have a direct effect upon one's life.

- The *Invocation* clears the soul committee, guides and guardian angels. Note that once in a while guides and guardian angels need to be cleared, removed or traded out for a different team. For instance, we sometimes collect too many guides and guardian angels, they are at a lower frequency than we are, or our own needs have changed and we need helpers with a different expertise. Do so by saying *"Educate, elevate, remove or replace as needed."*

- By harmonizing with the Divine Plan through the *Invocation*, you should receive answers that are not only "for highest and best good" (which the High Self/Soul Committee provides), but also LifeWeaves your answers with what is best for you or the client into the overall scheme of things.

CHAPTER 7

Basic LifeWeaving Protocol

Prepare for the Session

1. Prepare to work by clearing yourself and your surroundings.

2. Obtain permission to work on your patient by asking: *"May I?"* *"Can I?"* *"Should I?"*

3. Set up a healing grid around your patient and place a White Light tunnel between the two of you.

4. Harmonize your energy with that of the client.

Invocation to Clear the Client

Say to the client: "*Create a spinning* (either direction) *column of White Light around yourself, connecting one end to Unlimited Source and the other to the Healing Temple at the center of the Earth.*

Now invoke your mighty I AM presence and the Violet Flame of Transmutation to completely over light your body and being,

To align, clear, harmonize and balance your Personal Trinity, to clear your soul committee, guides and guardian angels, and to harmonize all with the Divine Plan."

Basic LifeWeaving Protocol

1. Use the **LifeWeaving** Worksheet *Check List for Preparedness* to confirm that the *Invocation* clearing was successful. Then ask *Supplemental Questions* as needed or desired.

2. Align your pendulum on the POWER *Chart Key* arrow, and using intention, 'add in' the client and the issue or statement to test, and dowse the *Chart Key* asking: "*What is needed to help?*" or another question of your choice.

3. Dowse the *Chart Key* and follow directions to the appropriate chart and/or sections, collecting (dowse for) any *Keyword(s)* and placing them in the 'holding basket' until the *Clearing Macro* is indicated. Continue to collect *Keywords* in each section you are dowsing until your pendulum remains at neutral on that section's neutral line.

4. Return to and dowse the *Chart Key* for the next action.

5. Always sending any results to the holding basket, continue testing sections of indicated charts until the pendulum moves to and indicates *Clearing Macro* on the *Chart Key*.

6. Spiral the contents of the holding basket through the body, mind and spirit while saying the *Clearing Macro* (found on the next page and on the RESEARCH CHART).

7. Do the *Completion Check* (found on page 65 and on the RESEARCH CHART) for the issue/statement you have just tested and cleared. Ask "*Is there anything else contributing to the issue, or that I should ask instead?*" "*Is this true for the client's Ego, Self, Soul and spirit helpers?*"

   Take any positive answers to the POWER *Chart Key* neutral line and test as usual (Steps 2-7) until the initial issue tests at neutrality.

   Next, use the *Completion Check* to confirm that the issue also is clear on all body levels, from the physical up through the spiritual.

8. To complete a healing, have the client spiral unconditional love (gold light with glitter) through his/her body, mind and spirit. This should usually be done after clearing a specific issue.

9. Send all the healing that has occurred during the session back through seven generations on both the mother's and father's sides to accomplish generational clearing. Follow that with more unconditional love.

Clearing Macro:

Bundle and spiral
(ALL WORDS THAT TESTED)
through the body, mind &
spirit; at all body levels,
frequencies, realities,
incarnations, dimensions,
and for all times;
plus all blocks, memories,
intent & healing.
Now flood with
unconditional love (gold
light with silver glitter).

Completion Check:

Is the issue clear for the
Trinity?
The Ego?
The Self?
The Soul?
Assigned spirits?

Is the issue clear on
all levels:
Physical?
Energetic?
Emotional?
Mental?
Spiritual?

Figure 22 *Clearing Macro* and *Completion Check*

Close the Session

1. Give thanks to all spiritual helpers who assisted during the session.

2. Close down the White Light tunnel, and disconnect yourself energetically from the client.

3. Suggest that the client renew his/her column of White Light, the Violet Flame and *I AM* presence.

CHAPTER 8

Advanced Protocols, Uses and Tips

These advanced clearing protocols give the LifeWeaver more direction for clearing specific issues - what to ask, what to look for and how to clear. Note that all use the *Basic LifeWeaving Protocol* presented in Chapter Seven.

After the general clearing (the eleven questions on the preparedness check list) is complete, any of these questions can be placed (using intention) on the POWER CHART neutral line along with the client and those involved and dowse. The protocols, special questions, follow up items or other things to be aware of are listed for each topic.

These are the topics covered:

- o   Animal Clearing
- o   Business or Service Clearing
- o   General Clearing Using Specific Sections of a Chart
- o   Health Issue Inquiry, General
- o   Health Issue or Symptom, Targeted Clearing
- o   Inanimate Object Clearing
- o   Original Perfect Destiny Blueprint Clearing
- o   Original Perfect Health Blueprint Clearing
- o   Past Life Research
- o   Present Life Research

- o   Relationship Clearing for Groups
- o   Relationship Clearing for Two People
- o   Timeline Clearing
- o   Upgrading Frequency in General

Animal Clearing

Uses: Solving pet issues such as clearing relationships between pets and owners; selecting a pet; figuring out what a pet needs; checking on health issues, supplements, etc.

Tips: Treat an animal the same as a person having a Soul Committee, Ego, Self and spirit helpers.

Protocol: Use the same protocol as for business or service clearing.

Business or Service Clearing

Uses: Job hunting; identifying and correcting business problems; deciding whether to use a particular business or service; testing whether you and a client are a good fit, etc.

Tips: Treat a business just as you would a living person, having a Soul Committee, Ego, Self and Soul, and spirit helpers. Also when dealing with a business entity, remember you will also need to include the owner/operator, board of directors, employees or any others related to its workings.

Protocol:

1. Obtain permission to work from the business entity and all others who will be part of the clearing.

2. Apply the *Invocation*. Note that you can do a "turbo clear" by applying the *Invocation* to each person who will be part of the session without needing to go through the clearing process step by step for each individual. Just confirm with a *"May I?" "Can I?"*, *"Should I?"* before bringing them up during the testing. Stop if you don't get permission.

3. Check the Level of Soul Consciousness of the business entity and any others involved.

4. Check "*% harmony, cooperation and agreement between all involved*" (the business entity and particular persons).

5. Put your pendulum over the neutral line of the POWER CHART and add in your question, the business entity, plus any others involved and do the *Basic LifeWeaving Protocol* as needed to bring all into neutrality.

6. When finished, test that each person and the business entity are in neutrality in any combination.

7. Ask *"Is there anything else needed for this group, contributing to the issue, or that I should ask instead?"*

8. Recite any new issues while your pendulum is in a gentle neutral swing over the neutral line of the POWER *Chart Key* and do the *Basic LifeWeaving Protocol* until all inquires have been cleared to neutrality and your questions are satisfied.

9. Close the session.

Follow-Up: You still might also need to do relationship clearing or group clearing as well. Also, be sure that everyone's guides/guardian angels are neutral with other spirit helpers in the group.

General Clearing Using Specific Sections of a Chart

Uses: For practice clearing or when there is no specific agenda.

Protocol:

1. Obtain permission to work on the client.

2. Apply the *Invocation.*

3. Select one section of the **LifeWeaving** POWER CHART to work on (*e.g., Section B - Mayan Levels of Consciousness*).

4. Place the client's *Personal Trinity* on the neutral line of the POWER *Chart Key* and mentally add in the first item to test (*e.g., Cellular*) and look for neutrality - meaning the item is clear. Use the *Basic LifeWeaving Protocol* to clear any positives.

5. Go on to the next item in the section you have chosen to clear (*e.g., Mammalian*) and process as needed until it tests neutral.

6. Continue until you have tested and cleared each item in the category to neutrality.

7. Read the closing statement.

Group Clearing

Uses: To help a number of people reach agreement on an issue; to test where a group is in the decision-making process; to identify where or with whom an emotional block resides; to identify the energy and consciousness of a group.

Tip: Whomever the answers are being asked for is added to the neutral line along with the question.

Tip: When checking for neutrality in the *Archetype Section C* of the POWER CHART, you can ask how one person sees (conscious level) and perceives (subconscious level) the others, either individually or as a group. You can also ask how he or she sees and perceives themselves within the group. By doing so any still-hidden feelings will be revealed. If anything other than neutrality comes up, place the person and the dowsed archetype on the neutral line of the POWER CHART and do more clearing until neutrality is finally reached.

Protocol:

1. Obtain permission to work from everyone in the group.
2. Apply the *Invocation* to all. (Ask for a 'turbo clear' – *i.e.,* that all parties involved are taken through the steps of the *Invocation* without you having to consciously work on each individual.) Also clear any spiritual connections between group members.
3. With your pendulum in a neutral swing over a neutral line and using intention, place one member on the line, then mentally or verbally add in each member of the group one by one. The pendulum should remain in a neutral swing each time. Note that these answers are from point of view of the person being cleared.

4. If the pendulum swings left off neutral, there is a program that needs to be cleared between them: Do the *Basic LifeWeaving Protocol* using the phrase *"Programs running between these two?"* on the *Chart Key* neutral line as your question. Note: if at any time the pendulum moves off neutral to the right of center (rather than to the left), the problem belongs to some of the spirit helpers. Clear them with **LifeWeaving** and/or say *"Educate, elevate, remove or replace as needed"* and retest.

   If there is still imbalance between them, ask: *"How many programs are running between these two clients?"* (Look for a number.)

   a) *"Turbo clear as many as possible."*
   b) *"How many programs are still running?"* (Get a number).
   c) Start with the POWER CHART and clear to neutrality.
   d) Continue until all programs between these individual clients are cleared.

5. Place a different member of the group on neutral and repeat Steps 3 and 4 to get that person's point of view. Continue this process until all members are neutral about each other.

6. Next, ask *"Is there any combination of group members that is not in balance?"* If yes, you need to find this combination. Treat and clear as needed until the pendulum remains in a neutral swing for any combination of those involved. (If it is a large group, it is helpful to write the names down on a sheet of paper in a semicircle so you can dowse them more efficiently.)

7. As a final check of each person's mental neutrality, place one or a combination of members on the neutral line of the *Archetypes Section C* and see what tests when adding in another person or the group as a whole. If a specific archetype or set of archetypes shows up, clear those using the *Basic LifeWeaving Protocol*. If the pendulum remains in a neutral swing, the group relationship clearing is complete.

8. At this point if you are checking for a group decision, you can also ask *"What percent is everyone's Personal Trinity in alignment, harmony and cooperation?"* Using **LifeWeaving**, bring them all as

close to 100% harmony before seeking answers to a business question.

9. Close the session.

Health Issue Inquiry (General)

Uses: To test general health; to identify and clear emotional blocks causing health-related issues; to identify what level a symptom is coming from so the root of the disease can be addressed; to identify past life cell memory affecting the body in this life, etc.

Tips: LifeWeaving can affect health on the physical level even though the method works more directly with the spiritual, energetic and emotional levels of the body. However, this method can still have a major effect on a person's physical body since once the block has been cleared, the physical has a better chance to heal. For greatest effect, if an illness is firmly entrenched on the physical level, add in a physical healing approach such as massage, acupuncture, herbs, energy work, etc. along with the **LifeWeaving**.

Protocol:

1. Obtain permission to work on the client.

2. Apply the *Invocation.*

3. Place the client and the question *"How can I help his/her health?"* on the POWER *Chart Key* neutral line and dowse.

4. Follow the *Basic LifeWeaving Protocol* and clear.

5. After clearing to neutrality, test *"Is there anything else needed for this person's health, contributing to it, or that I should ask about instead?"*

6. Recite any new issues while your pendulum is on the neutral line of the POWER *Chart Key*, watching for a break to the left off the neutral line indicating a positive, and doing *Basic LifeWeaving Protocol* until clear and satisfied.

7. Do the *Completion Check* and be sure that the issue is clear on all parts of the *Personal Trinity* - especially the physical self, which is

the hardest to clear for physical problems - as well as the other body levels.

8. Close the session.

Health Issue or Symptom (Targeted Clearing)

Uses: To find and clear emotional and energetic blocks that are part of a specific physical complaint; to reduce or clear pain; to identify the possible cause of the complaint; to identify contributing factors.

Tips:

- o Note that if you dowse the POWER *Chart Key* and are immediately directed to the PRSM DIAGNOSIS CHART, the health issue usually has a physical basis. If directed to stay on the POWER CHART or to go to the RESEARCH CHART first, the source of the physical complaint is probably being caused by emotional, mental, energetic or spiritual issues or combinations of them.
- o Be sure to establish what body level the problem resides on and clear the symptom or issue to neutrality on all levels.
- o Note that when dealing with health issues, the *Self* portion of the *Personal Trinity* may need additional clearing even though the *Trinity* on the whole tests as clear.
- o Ask *"Is this health issue part of the Divine Plan?"* If so, clear using *"Make the lesson easy"* as your statement.
- o Occasionally you might be directed to the PRSM CHART, *Section B Deaths.* This section helps identify the specifics of a past life death, or you can simply clear the entire chart without any research. Just ask to *"Clear all cellular memories of past life deaths."*

Protocol:

1. Obtain permission to work on the client.

2. Apply the *Invocation.*

3. Place the client and *"How can I help his/her [symptom]?"* (use the exact word or words the client uses to describe the problem) on the *Chart Key* neutral line and dowse.

4. Follow the *Basic LifeWeaving Protocol* and clear.

5. After clearing to neutrality, test *"Is there anything else needed for this person's [symptom]?"*

6. Recite any new issues while your pendulum is on the neutral line of the POWER *Chart Key* and do the *Basic LifeWeaving Protocol* until clear and satisfied.

7. Get feedback from the client if possible about how he/she would now describe the symptom. (*e.g.* 'pain' might become 'pressure' after a round or two of clearing).

8. Do basic **LifeWeaving** on the client by adding in the new description to the neutral line (*e.g.* 'pressure') and clearing to neutrality.

9. Do the *Completion Check* to be sure that the issue is clear on all body levels for the *Personal Trinity* and especially for the physical self, which is the hardest level to clear of physical problems. Also test that guides/guardian angels or other spirits are also clear and not influencing the client's health.

10. Place your pendulum on the POWER *Chart Key* neutral line, add in the client and begin substituting other words to describe the symptom. For example, for a sugar problem also test 'diabetes,' 'high blood sugar,' 'high glucose,' 'sugar issues,' 'insulin resistance,' etc. If any of these random words causes the pendulum to fall to the left off the neutral line, that statement needs to be cleared. Continue adding in anything that might be relevant to the symptom described and make sure the client remains neutral.

11. Recite any new issues while your pendulum is on the neutral line of the POWER *Chart Key* and do the *Basic LifeWeaving Protocol* until clear and satisfied.

12. Close the session.

Discussion: Physical problems usually respond nicely to **LifeWeaving** if the client is at a high enough level of consciousness (above 10). However, the pain or issue may return after a while due to the belief system that 'time is needed to heal.' Encourage the client to believe in miracles. Note that symptoms can return after the client leaves the strong presence and belief matrix of the practitioner.

Inanimate Object Clearing

Uses: Clearing a machine, house, automobile, etc.

Tips: Treat inanimate objects (*e.g.,* businesses, cars, houses, etc.) like a person, as if it has a Self, Soul and Ego, and proceed with the *Basic LifeWeaving Protocol.*

Original Perfect Destiny Blueprint Clearing

Uses: Helps a person to return to his/her originally planned destiny path.

Protocol:

1. Obtain permission to work on the client.

2. Apply the *Invocation.*

3. Test *"What % is the client harmonized with his/her original perfect destiny blueprint?"* If 100%, you are done. Go to step #8. If less than 100%, continue with #4-7.

4. On any number chart, test *"At what age was the client thrown off the original track?"*

5. On the RESEARCH CHART, test for *"What energy caused the derailment?"* and, if desired, *"Who caused the shift?"*

6. Return to the *Chart Key* neutral line, add in the client, age and energy or energies dowsed, and follow prompts to either add in any other information from the other sections or charts or to do the *Clearing Macro.*

7. Once all has been cleared to neutrality, recheck *"What % is the client aligned with his/her original perfect destiny blueprint?"* If at 100%, you are done. If less than 100%, return to step #4 and repeat clearing until the client is at 100%.

8. Close the session.

Original Perfect Health Blueprint Clearing

Uses: Helps a person return to his/her originally planned health path if they have been thrown 'off track.' However, remember that we sometimes program in disease or injury as part of our life lessons so the perfect health blueprint may not necessarily include perfect overall health during a lifetime.

Protocol:

1. Obtain permission to work on the client.

2. Apply the *Invocation.*

3. Test *"What % is the client still harmonized with his/her original perfect health blueprint?"* If 100%, you are done. If less than 100%, continue with #4.

4. *"What % is this in harmony with his or her soul's destiny this lifetime?"* If 100% aligned with the soul's work, you are done. If not at 100%, go to #5 to clear.

5. On any number chart, test at what age the client was thrown off the original track.

6. On the RESEARCH CHART, test what energy caused the derailment.

7. Return to the POWER *Chart Key* neutral line, add in the client, age and energy or energies dowsed; follow prompts to either add in any other information from the other sections or charts or to do the *Clearing Macro.*

8. Once all has cleared, recheck *"What % is the client aligned with his/her original perfect health blueprint?"* If at 100%, you are done. If less than 100%, return to steps #4-7 and repeat questions and clearing until the client is at 100%.

9. Close the session.

Past Life Research

Uses: Past life research is helpful if you want more details on any case.

Past life research often clarifies why certain relationship issues or specific health problems are coming up now for your client. These current problems may be a form of payback for previous encounters that went badly, or may explain current health problems due to the type of trauma or the age when a person underwent trauma in the past. Knowledge of past occurrences often helps a person understand and/or forgive what is taking place in this current life.

Tips: It can help to write down (in a semicircle or across a page) the name/description of everyone involved that comes up during the testing so you can dowse this list during the clearing.

Protocol:

1. Using the relationship portion of the RESEARCH CHART *Section A*, identify a list of all 'characters' involved when the program first established. Note that this is how the spirits see and name themselves. For example, female + grandparent = grandmother, male +religious figure = priest, grandparent + religious + male = 'pope' level leader of a religion), etc. (See the next section for help translating your findings.)

2. *"Was there hurt or harm?"* (yes or no). *"Slight, serious, or death?"*

3. (Optional) *"Type of harm?"* - found on the PRSM CHART - beheading, disease, torture, drowning, hanging, rape, burning, crucifixion, stoning, imprisonment, poisoning, religious sacrifice, starvation or other.

4. *"Which character was harmed?"* (Can be more than one)

5. *"Which character did it?"* (Can be more than one)

6. *"What roles are the characters' souls in this current lifetime?"* (Compare them to the client and anyone else that seems to be involved.

7. *"Was there any other hurt or harm?"* (research as needed) Note that it is not unusual for a character to harm another and then turn around and commit suicide.

8. Clear any *Keywords* as usual using the *Basic LifeWeaving Protocol.*

Determining the Characters for Past Life Research

Using the LIFEWEAVING Research Chart, *Section A - Relationships*, let your pendulum swing freely and allow as many *Keywords* to come up as possible. Then use your intuition to help interpret your results. The following are some examples:

- A grandparent is a person of stature and in authority. Therefore,
  - Grandparent + male/female = grandfather /grandmother
  - Grandparent + religious figure = the "pope" level of a religion
- A parent is a person with some authority. Therefore,
  - Parent + male/female = father/mother
  - Parent+ religious male/female = priest/priestess at the "bishop" level
- A child has little authority. Therefore,
  - Child + male/female = son or daughter
  - Child + religious male/female = novice priest/nun
- Add in other modifiers when they come up. For example:
  - Religious + sibling male = brother or monk
  - Religious + male = priest/brother/wizard
  - Religious + female = nun/witch
  - Religious + female + parent = head nun or witch
  - Dark energy + religious group = sorcery or dark witchcraft group
  - Guardian angel + female + spouse = a wife acting as guardian angel to her partner

Present Life Research

Uses: Present life research can clarify why certain relationship issues or specific health problems are coming up now for your client. It can help pinpoint what age an issue precipitated and identify other persons or family members involved. For example, present life research can find that a man sees all women as victims because at the age of five years old, he saw or heard his father treating or calling all women 'victims.' At this point you can clear both the son and the father's spirit (if permission to work is first established with the father's soul).

Tips: It can help to write down (in a semicircle or across the page) the name/description of everyone involved that comes up during the testing so you can dowse this list during the clearing protocol.

Protocol:

1. *"What age did the program or issue establish this lifetime?"*

2. *"Who is involved?"*

3. *"Was there hurt or harm?"*

4. *"Slight, serious or death?"* (Note that a child may register serious physical or emotional harm as "death").

5. (Optional) *"What type of harm?"* (From the PRSM CHART, *Section B.)*

6. *"Who was harmed?"*

7. *"Who did it?"*

8. *"Was there any other hurt or harm?"* (Repeat steps four to seven as needed.)

9. Clear as usual.

Relationship Clearing for Two People

Uses: To test compatibility between two people and to see how they consciously and subconsciously relate; to find and clear karmic and other issues between a couple; to help determine if a person would be a good mate, coworker, friend; to identify spiritual connections between two people, etc.

Protocol:

1. Obtain permission to work from both persons involved in the clearing.

2. Apply the *Invocation* to both. (You can ask for a 'turbo clear', *i.e.,* that both parties automatically receive all steps of the *Invocation* and clearing.)

3. Using the worksheet, check that the *Invocation* completed all the clearing it was supposed to do. Then check the Level of Soul Consciousness and energy of each.

4. Check for spiritual connections between the two.

   o *"Same soul and flame family?"*
   o *"Siamese Twin?"* (working close together but from different soul families).
   o *"Any karmic issues between them?"*
   o *"Any cords or attachments between them?"*
   o *"Any curses, contracts, heart vows, hidden vows or soul programs running between them?"*
   o *"Are they working together spiritually (as guardian angels)?"*

5. Do basic **LifeWeaving** on any of the above items that need cleared.

6. Use the POWER CHART *Section C Archetypes* and ask *"How does each see the other?"* (Do this individually.) (This is conscious thought.)

7. Use the POWER CHART *Section C Archetypes* and ask *"How do they perceive each other?"* (Do this individually.) (This is subconscious thought.)

8. Use the POWER CHART *Archetypes Section C* and ask *"How does one see him/her self when with the other person?" "How does one perceive him/her self when with the other person?"*

9. Ask *"Is there anything else to clear between these two, contributing to, or that I should ask instead?"*

10. *"Is there anything buried, stuffed or saved between them that needs cleared?"*

11. Ask *"Is there anything between their guides and/or guardian angels that needs cleared?"*

12. Recite any new issues while your pendulum is on the neutral line of the POWER *Chart Key* and look for disharmony (the pendulum drops off the neutral line) and do the *Basic LifeWeaving Protocol* until clear and satisfied.

13. Close the session.

Timeline Clearing

Uses: To identify a particular age and experience when an emotional block originated; to be sure that a block won't appear at the same age during a lifetime; to pinpoint a blocking issue at various ages.

Tips: It is easiest to start the clearing by asking about years 1-10, 11-20, 21-30, etc. until you reach a decade that shows a blockage - and the pendulum moves off left of the neutral line. Then test one year at a time in that decade, *e.g.,* 21, 22, 23, 24, etc., until the answer is found.

Protocol:

o **Entire Lifetime** - Place the harmonized *Personal Trinity* and your pendulum in a gentle swing along the neutral line on a chart; then using intention add in ages at whatever parameter you wish to test (hours, days, weeks, months, years, etc.) up to the maximum time you wish to check. Research and clear any imbalance as it comes up with the *Basic LifeWeaving Protocol* and clear the client to an *"infinite age in that lifetime."*

o **Specific Age** - Sometimes as you do **LifeWeaving** clearing, a particular age will come up for more than one problem. If this happens, after you have completed that clearing, research that age and look for and clear any other problems connected to it.

o **Past Life Time Lock** - As you clear a timeline, you should also check whether the age is also locked in a past life. Sometimes a person gets 'stuck' at a particular age in a past life due to a traumatic experience and is still operating at that blockage level, even in his or her current life. Be sure the person clears to an "infinite age" in the past life, and at least up to their current age in this one. Better yet, clear them to infinity in the current life as well.

Upgrading Frequency in General

Uses: To help ease the physical pain and symptoms brought on by the ascension process; to find hidden issues that can be cleared.

Tips: Upgrading the frequency can be applied to the body in general or to specific parts of the body, emotions or energy. The solutions may include simple clearing, adding in supplements, colors, activities, etc. Just follow the prompts working with the *Chart Keys* to identify, clear and upgrade as needed. Note that this type of work can be done often, especially as we are changing so fast during this phase of the ascension process.

Protocol:

1. Obtain permission to work on the client.

2. Apply the *Invocation*.

3. Place the client and *"How can I help upgrade his/her frequency?"* on the POWER *Chart Key* neutral line and dowse.

4. Follow the *Basic LifeWeaving Protocol* and clear.

5. After clearing these to neutrality, ask *"Is there anything else needed to upgrade this person's frequency, anything contributing to it, or that I should ask about instead?"*

6. Recite any new issues while your pendulum is on the neutral line of the POWER *Chart Key* and look for any imbalance, indicated if the pendulum falls off to the left of neutral. Do the *Basic LifeWeaving Protocol* until all are cleared to neutrality and you and the client are satisfied.

7. Do the *Completion Check* making sure that the issue is clear on all body levels for the *Personal Trinity* and especially the physical self, which is the hardest to clear.

8. Close the session.

CHAPTER 9

The All-Important Questions

Questioning in General

When dowsing, the integrity of the answers depends on what questions are asked and how they are asked. Some things to watch for when forming your questions are the following:

- **Be Clear and Concise!** For example, *"Will I be successful?"* is a poor question unless you know specifically what the term "success" means to you or your client. In another example, if you have a strong belief in the existence of past lives, your High Self may not always differentiate between this current life and past ones so you must be crystal clear with your questions and intent by asking *"Am I a healer in this current life?"*, rather than *"Am I a healer?"*

- **Ask One Question at a Time.** A poor example is Q: *'Did so and so hurt me on purpose?"* Instead, ask two separate questions: Q: *'Did so and so hurt me?"* and Q: *'Did he/she do it on purpose?"*

- **Keep Your Verbal Question Identical to the Question in Your Mind.** If you work too fast you can confuse yourself. Slow down.

- **Confirming an Answer.** Double check an answer by re-stating the question in a different way. For example, Q: *"Do I currently live in Arizona?"* A: *"Yes."* To recheck the answer, restate the question as: *"Do I currently live in any other state than Arizona?"* A: *"No."* Now you have double confirmation.

Interpretation of Answers

- Answers cannot always be taken literally!

- If you get a questionable answer, re-phrase the question or ask for more information to clarify it.

- Predictions made by dowsing cannot really be trusted.

- If your mind has already been made up before you dowse, the answer will come out exactly as you expected (and is probably wrong).

Checking the Accuracy of Answers

1. Once in a while when your pendulum is in a "*yes*" swing, quickly slip in the question: "*Is this a lie?*"

2. If the pendulum response shows any hesitation at all or is slow to swing over into a "*no*" pattern (going in the opposite direction), stop and check where the answers are coming from.

3. If the pendulum does swing quickly into the "*no*" pattern, next ask "*Is this a lie?*" If the pendulum remains in the "*no*" position, you have just received double confirmation that your answer is correct.

4. You can also ask "*Are the answers infinitely correct?*" to expose answers that may only be partially correct.

Selecting Questions to Ask

There are several good sources for the questions used during a LifeWeaving session:

- **Protocols**. Some recommended statements or questions to work with can be found in the various protocols presented in this book.

- **The Client**. Listen carefully to the client during the intake interview. Look for phrases or statements that seem to hold special significance. For example: *"I tend to go ballistic...," "I shut down...," "I don't feel I will live very long...," "Everyone who looks at me knows...,"* etc.

By **LifeWeaving** these statements, the practitioner can often trace back to the root cause of a deep emotional blockage and clear it, thus helping the client make a breakthrough. Always go back to the original phrase you have been addressing and confirm that it is has cleared. In order to remember the exact phrase you started working on, jot it down on your worksheet.

- **Words That Come Up Frequently During Clearing**. As you do **LifeWeaving** clearing with a client, be alert for specific words or archetypes that surface often as you work. For example, if the queen archetype comes up four times during the general tune-up and life area clearing, it is a good idea to go back and put the client on neutral, add in the word (in this example, the queen archetype), and LifeWeave the phrase or words until it tests at neutrality.

- **Intuitive Sense**. The practitioner can follow his/her intuition during the session, **LifeWeaving** into other areas and questions as indicated. The key is that after following these intuitive clues, the healer should always go back to the original statement being worked on and check whether clear or not.

- **RESEARCH CHART, *Section A Questions***. Any problem can be analyzed by testing it against each question listed in this section.

Questions for Specific Problems

Client is always attracting world energies or entities:

- *"How to best help this client stop attracting energies, entities, cords, etc.?"*

Client does not feel any change after a session:

- *"What percent of the issue belongs to the client?" "To the client's spirit helpers?" "To others?" "Are those others incarnated, spirit or both?"*

- *"What is the best way to help this client clear the issue?"*

- *"What is the best way to clear whatever is preventing this client from healing?"*

- *"What percent does this person believe that the **LifeWeaving** method can help them?"* (Clear to 100% if possible.)

- *"Are there benefit programs causing the client to hold on to his or her problem?"*

Relationship clearing does not work:

- *"Between these two people, are there any left-over curses, contracts, heart vows, hidden vows or soul programs?"*

- *"With what archetype(s) do these people see each other consciously?"*

- *"With what archetype(s)do these people see each other subconsciously?"*

- *"With what archetype(s) does this person consciously see him or herself when with the other?"*

- *"Is there a need for forgiveness and apology?"*

- *"Are both sets of spirit helpers in harmony, cooperation and agreement, free of any programs?"*

Similar issues come up immediately after completing a clearing (indicating a new layer is ready to clear):

- *"Show me how to best help the next layer(s) of the issue."*

- *"What percent do these issues belong to the client?"*

- *"What percent do these issues belong to assigned spirit helpers?"*

- *"What percent do these issues belong to others, either incarnated, spirit or both?"*

CHAPTER 10

LifeWeaving Problems and Solutions

LifeWeaving can be very effective but is not perfect for everyone or every situation - no one method or technique is a perfect fit to correct all problems for all people. The following information gives the major areas where the efficacy of the LifeWeaving system can be compromised.

Issues with the Client

1. **Low consciousness level**: If the client is at a lower level of consciousness, his or her perception, doubts and density can prevent improvement from happening.

   Solution: To identify this type of person, find his/her level of soul consciousness using any number chart. If it reads below the 6th or 7th dimension (*i.e.*, testing at number 6 or 7) it is better to either refer out or work with these clients using a more tangible, physical approach like massage, chiropractic, or surgery.

2. **Little or no belief in the LifeWeaving clearing system**: When the client's belief in this type of healing work is limited or absent.

   Solution: Clear the client to 100% belief if possible using the *Basic LifeWeaving Protocol* and a statement like: *'Improving poor belief in the effectiveness of LifeWeaving.'*

3. **Patient identifies with his/her problem and subconsciously doesn't want to improve**. After a long health issue, a person can become so focused on a problem, he/she fails to notice that there has been improvement. Some people even go so far as to identify

so much with the illness, that they cannot see themselves in any other light.

Solution #1: Keep records such as range of motion, system surveys, etc. that qualify or quantify function so both patient and practitioner can measure improvement.

Solution #2: Start asking the client "*What type of changes did you notice?*" rather than "*How do you feel?*"

4. **Temporary improvement followed by a relapse.** The client improves during the session and for a time afterwards but then relapses. There are several possible solutions to this problem.

Solution #1: The client needs to make an effort to change his/her lifestyle, actions or thoughts, working to maintain wellness and keeping vibrational frequency and level of consciousness at a high level.

Solution #2: The practitioner should check for another layer of the problem or for other contributing factors that need to be cleared.

Solution #3: Because both of these aspects tend to hold on to physical problems, (1) test the physical layer of the body separately from the body levels as a whole, and (2) test the Self separately from the *Personal Trinity.*

Solution #4: The client needs more sessions. However, if there has been no change after two or three sessions, try a different approach or refer the client out.

Solution #5: A more physical approach to healing needs to be added as part of the treatment plan.

Solution #6: Try a different line of questioning. Abandon the line of questions dealing with symptoms, and instead pursue the questions like *"Why does change not occur?"* or *"Why does the clearing not hold?"* or *"Why does the client need this problem?"*

Issues with the Practitioner

1. **The Practitioner is distracted.**

Solution: The intentions of the LifeWeaver must be focused on the treatment at hand so it is best if he or she works in a quiet, protected setting.

2. **The LifeWeaver's thinking is too linear**. The many layers, twists and turns that the LifeWeaving process can take definitely affect the success of a treatment, and the LifeWeaver must be flexible enough to follow them. During a typical session, the practitioner addresses specific symptoms, issues or statements. Next he or she may choose to LifeWeave a specific organ or chakra because it comes up as the location of many of the blocks during the clearing work. The practitioner may then decide to investigate a specific age that comes up often during a session and clear it, or next might feel the need to do past life clearing to understand the details of a problem better.

Solution: The practitioner should always keep an open, investigative mind that flows with the energy during the clearing and is able to follow leads and intuitive thoughts as they come up.

A Need for a Physical Approach

1. **A problem is manifesting heavily in the physical body level**. As mentioned before, there is often still a need to address the physical body directly due to its density.

Solution: Select a physical approach to help the body heal more effectively.

Allow for Miracles

Note that miracles can happen instantaneously without applying any physical healing method, but most practitioners and clients have a very deeply ingrained belief that healing takes time to happen and this belief is almost impossible to overcome. To help, try 'brainwashing' your clients into accepting that miracles can happen and healing can be instantaneous. Plant the seed for them to expect change as well as improvement.

CHAPTER 11

Case Histories

The following LifeWeaving sessions help illustrate this clearing work on actual clients with a variety of issues. In presenting these cases, I have emphasized the questions asked rather than answers dowsed in an attempt to show the thought process involved in the clearings. The case discussion at the end of each report points out the discoveries found during the sessions. The format I have used includes the following:

History/Symptoms: Some of the background information on the client and issue, including specific statements made by the clients during our discussion or on their e-mails.

Tune-Up and Balancing: Essentially this checks that the *Invocation* did what it was supposed to do to prepare the client for the session.

Supplemental Questions: Selected from the list on the worksheet.

Specific Testing Questions: This starts the targeted clearing work for issues that the client brought up.

Discussion: Points of interest to help explain the clearing.

Follow-Up: Information concerning changes received from the client following a session.

Note that any positive findings were cleared using LifeWeaving during the sessions.

CASE ONE: Back Pain

August 2011

History/Symptoms: Female in her 50's with chronic back pain; abdominal surgery seven years prior followed by a life-threatening infection. Her medical doctor is now suggesting she get more surgery done. During our intake discussion, the client talked about "having difficulty when leaning forward" as well as used the term "cracked vertebrae." The client also had questions about two different alternative health practitioners she was thinking of seeing. Work was done over the telephone as a distance clearing session.

Tune-Up and Balancing: Okay except for one intrusion (a psychic wound).

Supplemental Questions: Level of consciousness = 12.7; slow track soul.

Specific Testing Questions:

- *"Back issues in general?"* (testing the *Personal Trinity* on the physical level) = cleared programs on the physical, emotional, mental and spiritual levels. Astral level tested neutral (clear).

- *"Effects of previous surgery?"* = cleared on the physical and emotional body levels. Other levels were neutral.

- *"Suggested surgery on the whole area?"* = neutral all levels.

- *"Suggested surgery on a smaller area?"* = neutral all levels.

- *"Leaning forward?"* = programs on the emotional level were cleared; neutral on the other body levels.

- *"Cracked vertebrae?"* = cleared programs on the physical and spiritual levels; tested neutral for astral, emotional and mental levels.

- *"Practitioner One?"* = level of soul consciousness 11th dimension, 3rd octave (11.3); no spiritual connection to client; no karmic issues with client; would bring "health" energy to the client.

- *"Practitioner Two?"* = level of soul consciousness at 9th dimension, 11th octave (9.11); no spiritual connection to client; no karmic programs with client; would bring "acceptance and achievement" energy to the client.

Discussion: The client's high level of consciousness indicated she would do well with LIFEWEAVING work. The back pain did have some roots on the physical level so a physical healing approach like acupuncture was especially helpful. She also had mental and emotional blocks that had to be cleared to allow her back to heal.

Both potential practitioners were at a high enough level of consciousness to be good choices since there were no active karmic programs or spiritual connections between the client and them, but Practitioner One has the edge according to this testing with a higher level of consciousness and bringing in the energy of "health."

Follow-Up: Following the **LifeWeaving** session, the client's back physically felt much looser and she was in less pain. Currently she is seeing the acupuncturist for more physical support.

CASE 2: Child Frightened at Night

September 2011

History/Symptoms: 5 year old boy, frightened during the night when he heard whispering voices in his bedroom. His mother recommended that he send them "to the light" and tell them to leave him alone but that has not helped the situation. Note that the family lives across the street from a civil war cemetery.

Tune-Up and Balancing: Okay.

Supplemental Questions: Level of soul consciousness is 10.7.

Specific Testing Questions:

- *"People whispering at night?"* = neutral on the physical and mental levels; programs were identified and cleared on the astral and spiritual levels.

- *"Who is whispering?"* = I tested entities, *separates* and *discarnate* groups.

- *"Why are they there?"* = cleared several programs for the spirits.

- *"How is the land?"* = cleared a curse block.

- *"How do the entities view the child?"* = cleared the companion archetype and the *Keyword* of "acceptance" for the spirits.

Discussion: The child, whose parents are openly metaphysical, is an advanced (old) soul who is very aware of the spiritual realm around him. For this case clearing was mostly needed for the spirits, helping them to complete on this earth and finally cross over.

Follow-Up: The child created his own ceremony of mentally patrolling the perimeter of his room and placing lanterns around it. He is now sleeping fine.

CASE 3: Buying a House

October 2011

History: A couple is trying to buy a house but having issues with the bank seeming to block the short sale. Their main question is whether to let go of this house and continue looking. Wife is also experiencing exhaustion - wanting to nap all the time - and has a sore throat.

Tune-Up and Balancing: For both husband and wife - okay; for the bank and realtors - okay.

Supplemental Questions: Levels of consciousness - husband 10.0; wife 10.9; realtor 8.9; bank 3.2; banker they are dealing with 3.1.

Power Chart Testing in General: Cleared all involved for some general programs.

Specific Testing Questions used:

- *"Wife's throat pain and exhaustion?"* = ascension issues cleared.

- *"Wife and the house?"* = cleared programs on her physical, energetic and mental levels.

- *"Husband and the house?"* = neutral.

- *"The 'bank entity'?"* = no karmic programs with the couple; sees them as the servant archetype; sees the house as slave archetype.

- *"Wife letting the house go?"* = neutral on the physical, astral and mental levels. Cleared programs on both the emotional and spiritual levels.

- *"Husband letting go of the house?"* = neutral.

- *"Husband letting go of the large shop on the property?"* = programs cleared on all levels.

- *"Wife looking for a new house?"* = cleared mental level programs.

- *"Husband looking for a new house?"* = neutral.

- *"Pulling out of the deal on the house?"* = tests as 50% likely the bank would relent and move faster on the closing process.

- *"Banker relenting if they pull out of the deal?"* = cleared all levels.

Discussion: After the clearing work, it tested as highest option to pull out of the deal and look for another house.

Follow-Up: The couple found another house to buy but when the bank saw the offer being withdrawn on the first home, found a way to make the sale happen in a reasonable time frame.

CASE 4: Dementia

October 2011

History/Symptoms: Gentleman in his 80's diagnosed with early dementia. Very controlling at home with his wife and son. His medical doctor is keeping the dementia a secret from him.

Tune-Up and Balancing: Ok.

Supplemental Questions:

- Tested as having two concurrent lives.

- Level of consciousness at 7.1.

- POWER CHART testing in general: Cleared several *Mayan levels of Consciousness.*

Specific Testing Questions:

- *"Dementia?"* = cleared several programs on the physical, energetic, emotional, mental and spiritual levels.

- *"Early dementia?"* = cleared several programs on the physical, energetic, emotional, and mental levels as well as the affirmation about "deserving" (affirmation is from the POWER CHART).

- *"Being controlling?"* = cleared programs on the physical, emotional and spiritual levels. (Energetic and mental levels were neutral.)

- *"Controlling all women?"* = cleared issues on the physical and mental levels. The remainder were neutral.

- *"Controlling his wife?"* = cleared all levels.

- *"How his mind views his wife?"* = neutral.

- *"Women in general?"* = neutral.

Discussion: After clearing dementia programs for this gentlemen, he still tested as being affected by the word (putting the pendulum on neutral, adding in all his body levels and the word "dementia"). At this point I checked the second life he was concurrently incarnated in and found that in that incarnation he had full dementia. I tested that he should not be pulled out of the second life so to reduce the effects of that dementia in this life, I closed down the energy link between his two lives as much as possible and placed a strong filter on the link between those incarnations to protect him in this life.

Follow-Up: A month later, the client's neighbor still shows signs of dementia - still paranoid with his wife as his primary target and her never knowing what will set him off. My testing shows that the session was only 30% effective; his level of consciousness was the same. The dementia still tests in his alternate life and the connection between the two lives is 50% open again. No follow up **LifeWeaving** session was done.

At this point it is possible that more clearing sessions might help over time but with no guarantee.

CASE 5: Problems with a New Job

September 2011

History/Symptoms: "Started new job . . . help!" This person is a counselor with many years of experience and education but had been out of the job market for several years due to health issues. Now ready to return to work, she was hired for a counseling job for which she was overqualified. Shortly after starting, her life was put in danger because co-workers did not back her up during an incident with a dangerous client.

Tune-Up and Balancing: Okay. (Note that all involved in this clearing—including people and the business - were at least "turbo cleared" at the beginning of the session by applying the *Invocation*).

Supplemental Questions:

- Client's level of consciousness is 11.4 out of a possible 12.12.

- Job level of consciousness is 6.2.

- The building where the job was located has a 4.5 level of consciousness.

- The boss? = level of consciousness is 7.0.

- Other people at work average 6.7 level of consciousness.

Power Chart Testing in General:

- Cleared the client's *Personal Trinity*, guardian angels and guides for some issues. She is 100% in harmony with the job.

- Cleared the job and its assigned spirits for several programs.

- *"The building where the job is?"* = neutral for programs.

- *"The people at work?"* = cleared several issues in general. On average, the employees are 50% in harmony with the High Self of the business and 10% in harmony with my client's High Self.

Specific Testing Questions:

- *"Client and her new job?"* = cleared a few issues.

- *"Client and the building?"* = neutral.

- *"Client and her co-workers?"* = neutral from my client's point of view. (I checked for programs between any combination of them.)

- *"Co-workers and my client?"* = they saw her as the shadow engineer archetype (a master manipulator for her own needs) with energy about acceptance. Testing further, it was the co-workers who felt that the client would not accept them due to having less training.

- *"Everyone's assigned spirit helpers?"* = neutral. (I checked for programs between any combination of them.)

- *"The boss and my client?"* = testing the POWER CHART *Section C Archetypes,* the boss' mind categorizes the client as neutral. The boss views herself as shadow engineer archetype (a master manipulator for her own needs). The boss was not running any karmic programs or had any spiritual connection to the client.

Other Factors? =

- *"Best archetype for client to take on when interacting with her co-workers?"* = the companion (offering loyalty and support).

- *"Best archetype for client to take with her boss?"* = be neutral and adjust to the situation as needed.

- *"What lesson is this job bringing to my client?"* = acceptance and wholeness.

- *"What lesson is the client bringing to the job?"* = acceptance and trust.

- *"Anything Else?"* = using the POWER CHART, I found and cleared a 5th dimensional program that showed up at this stage.

Discussion: For this clearing, all participants including the business itself, needed to be cleared. The job was not the best fit for my client (4th highest option with #1 being the best) but it provided a means of financial support in her life during a time when jobs were scarce. However, her boss, all the other employees and the business itself were at a much lower level of consciousness which made the atmosphere that much harder to experience. Note that the population this business served averaged a 4.0 level of consciousness. This is a logarithmic range so overall this position was a tremendous stretch for my client's soul to try to work at.

Follow-Up: After the clearing, this client sought better support from her boss and co-workers and tried to make the job work but the work climate did not change. She pulled out quickly after another incident and has since found a much better work position.

CHAPTER 12

Practice LifeWeaving Exercises

To make the most of LifeWeaving, you can use the charts in several different ways to keep yourself clear, to clear others, to harmonize relationships, and to clear pets or businesses. The one requirement to accomplish these fantastic things is to actually use it, practice often and let your intuition guide you. The following are a few ways to practice.

Simple Clearing - to start your day or as needed during the day:

1. Say the *Invocation* to protect and align yourself, your *Personal Trinity*, your guardian angels and guides to the Divine Plan, and to obtain permission to work.

2. Place your pendulum into a neutral swing on the neutral line of the POWER *Chart Key* and ask *"What needs to be cleared?"* Collect any *Keywords* into an imaginary basket and send them through the *Clearing Macro* when it is indicated, then. Keep clearing until your pendulum remains in a neutral swing when asking the question.

3. Ask, *"Is there anything else?"* and clear whatever arises.

4. Once the pendulum remains at neutral and no other *Keywords* or clearing is indicated, do the *Completion Check*.

Clearing Specific Sections of a Chart

1. Read the *Invocation* and prepare yourself to work.

2. Select one section of the POWER CHART to work on (*e.g., Section B, Mayan Levels of Consciousness*).

3. Place your *Personal Trinity* on the neutral line of the *Chart Key* and mentally add in the first item to test (*e.g.,* Cellular) and look for neutrality (where the pendulum remains in a neutral swing over the neutral line - meaning the item is clear.) If not, do the *Basic LifeWeaving Protocol* and find all the *Keywords* that need to go through the *Clearing Macro* until neutrality is achieved.

4. Go on to the next item in the section you have chosen to clear (*e.g., Mammalian*) and process as needed until it tests neutral. Continue until you have tested and cleared each item in the Mayan section.

5. Do the *Completion Check*.

As you become more familiar with the charts and more confident with **LifeWeaving** clearing, you can begin working on others. However, as with any dowsing or energetic healing method, answers should always be examined using common sense and occasionally need to be confirmed by other methods, especially when dealing with physical symptoms.

Bibliography

Aivanhov, Omraam Mikhael

   A NEW EARTH---METHODS, EXERCISES, FORMULAS AND PRAYERS 4TH EDITION, COMPLETE WORKS - VOLUME 13 (France: Editions Prosveta, 1992)

Archangel Ariel and Tashira Tachi-ren

   WHAT IS LIGHTBODY? (Little Springs, Georgia: World Tree Press, 1999)

Blackburn, Gabriele

   SCIENCE AND THE ART OF PENDULUM---A COMPLETE COURSE IN RADIESTHESIA (Ojai, CA: Idywild Books, 1983)

Bletzer, June G., Ph.D.

   THE DONNING INTERNATIONAL ENCLYCLOPEDIC PSYCHIC DICTIONARY (West Chester, Pennsylvania: Whitford Press, 1986)

Brennan, Barbara A.

   HANDS OF LIGHT---A GUIDE TO HEALING THROUGH THE HUMAN ENERGY FIELD (NYC, NY: Bantam Books, 1987)

Capra, Fritjof

   THE TAO OF PHYSICS (Berkely: Shambala Press, 1975)

Cohen, Neil S.

   ATTITUDINAL AWARENESS GUIDE---EMOTIONAL / ATTITUDINAL CAUSES OF PHYSICAL PROBLEMS (Mount Shasta, CA: Legion of Light Products, 1989)

Conlon, Carole

   A MANUAL FOR 5TH DIMENSIONAL HEALING---LIFEWEAVING THE SPIRIT (Albuquerque, NM: AyniWrite Press 2008)

Conlon, Carole

   PRSM PENDULUM RESEARCH SOURCING METHOD---LIFEWEAVING THE BODY (Albuquerque, NM: AyniWrite Press 2009) de Flores, Bryan

MASTERWORKS (Las Vegas, Nevada: LightQuest International, 2006)

Detzler, Robert

SOUL RE-CREATION---DEVELOPING YOUR COSMIC POTENTIAL (Redmond, WA: SRC Publishing, 1994)

Detzler, Robert

YOUR MIND-NET, REPROGRAMMING THE SUBSCONSCIOUS (Redmond, WA: SRC Publishing, 1988)

Friedman, Norman

BRIDGING SCIENCE AND SPIRIT---COMMON ELEMENTS IN DAVID BOHM'S PHYSICS, THE PERENNIAL PHILOSOPHY AND SETH (St. Louis, MO: Living Lake Books, 1990)

Funk & Wagnalls

STANDARD DICTIONARY OF THE ENGLISH LANGUAGE INTERNATIONAL EDITION, VOL. I & II (New York: Funk & Wagnalls Publishing Co., Inc., 1973)

Grabhorn, Lynn

DEAR GOD! WHAT'S BEEN HAPPENING TO US? (Charlottesville, VA: Hampton Roads Publishing Co., Inc., 2003)

Hall, Manly P.

HEALING: THE DIVINE ART (Los Angeles, CA: Philosophical Research Society, 1995)

Hawkins, David R., M.D.

POWER VS. FORCE---AN ANATOMY OF CONSCIOUSNESS THE HIDDEN DETERMINANTS OF HUMAN BEHAVIOR (Sedona, AZ: Veritas Publishing, 1995)

Hawkins, David R., M.D.

THE EYE OF THE I---FROM WHICH NOTHING IS HIDDEN (Sedona, AZ, Veritas Publishing, 2001)

Hawkins, David R, M.D.

I: REALITY AND SUBJECTIVITY (Sedona, AZ: Veritas Publishing, 2003)

Leadbeater, C.W.

MAN VISIBLE INVISIBLE---EXAMPLES OF DIFFERENT TYPES OF MEN AS SEEN BY MEANS OF TRAINED CLAIRVOYANCE (Wheaton, IL: The Theosophical Publishing House, 1925)

Leadbeater, C.W.

THE INNER LIFE (Wheaton, IL: Theosophical Publishing House, 1978)

Leadbeater, C.W. & Besant, A.

THOUGHT-FORMS (Wheaton, Il: Theosophical Publishing House, 1971)

Longren, Sig

THE PENDULUM KIT (NYC, NY: Simon & Schuster, Inc., 1990)

Luppi, Diana and Mission Control

E.T. 101, THE COSMIC INSTRUCTION MANUAL (Santa Fe, NM: Intergalactic Council Publications, 1990)

Kinnear, Willis (ed)

SPIRITUAL HEALING---THE ART AND SCIENCE OF MEDITATION (Los Angeles, CA: Science of Mind Publications, 1983)

McLaren, Karla

YOUR AURA AND YOUR CHAKRAS---THE OWNER'S MANUAL (Dehli, India: Motilal Banarsidass Publ., 2000)

Monte, Tom and the Editors of East-West Natural Health

WORLD MEDICINE---THE EAST WEST GUIDE TO HEALING YOUR BODY (NYC, NY: Putnam Publishing Group, 1993)

Myss, Caroline

SACRED CONTRACTS, AWAKENING YOUR DIVINE POTENTIAL (New York: Harmony Books, 2001)

Neil, Penny R.N., M.S. (Ed.)

CONTACT REFLEX ANALYSIS AND APPLIED TROPHOLOGY---A HEALING ART RESEARCHED, DEVELOPED AND TAUGHT BY DR. D.A. VERSENDAAL (1976)

Nielson, Greg

BEYOND PENDULUM POWER: ENTERING THE ENERGY WORLD (Reno, NV: Conscious Books, 1988)

Nielson, Greg and Polansky, Joseph

PENDULUM POWER (Rochester, VT: Destiny Books, 1977)

Newton, Michael, Ph.D.

JOURNEY OF SOULS---CASE STUDIES OF LIFE BETWEEN LIVES (St. Paul, Minnesota: Llewellyn Publications, 1996)

Olson, Dale

ADVANCED PENDULUM INSTRUCTION AND APPLICATIONS VOL. 1 (Eugene, OR: Crystalline Publications, 1991)

Starr, Jelaila

WE ARE THE NIBIRUANS---RETURN OF THE 12TH PLANET BOOK ONE (The Nibiruan Council, 2003)

Talbot, Michael

HOLOGRAPHIC UNIVERSE (New York: Harper Perennial, Division of Harper Collins Publishers, 1991)

Wallace, Amy and Henkin, Bill

THE PSYCHIC HEALING BOOK (Oakland, CA: Wingbow Press, 1978)

Villoldo, Ph.D., Alberto

MENDING THE PAST AND HEALING THE FUTURE WITH SOUL RETRIEVAL (California: Hay House, Inc., 2005)

Index

ABOUT THE AUTHOR

Carole Conlon, M.T. (ASCP), L.Ac., holds the NCCAOM national board certification as Diplomate of Acupuncture. Following a 1984 graduation from the Northwest Institute of Acupuncture and Oriental Medicine in Seattle and an internship at the Chongqing Institute of Traditional Chinese Medicine in Chongqing, China, Carole worked as an acupuncturist in Washington State for 21 years. During that time she eventually specialized in Nogier's Auriculomedicine method.

Prior to her acupuncture studies, Carole worked as a registered medical technologist in a variety of hospital settings for 12 years, including five years serving in Barrow and Bethel Alaska Indian Health Service Hospitals. Carole also earned a Master's degree in Management and Supervision in the Health Care Field through Central Michigan University.

During the time Carole practiced traditional acupuncture, she also began developing a pendulum testing and healing method called LifeWeaving. Then in 2006, a paradigm-shifting course revealed her life destiny and in order to better embrace that mission, Carole began to upgrade and transform both herself and the pendulum method and started working more on an energetic, emotional and spiritual approach with patients.

Through LifeWeaving, Carole is able to re-code and re-calibrate a person's mental and emotional bodies in order to reverse and eliminate patterns of fear, karma, limitation, and self-sabotage. This method results in increased harmony, freedom from suffering and a marvelous synchronicity with all aspects of life and eases the transition into the coming Golden Age.

Now residing in New Mexico, Carole uses auricular acupuncture, nutritional counseling, *LifeWeaving* clearing, teaching and writing to help clients improve their own core health and wellbeing by restoring their ayni - their sacred relationship - with themselves, with each other, with the environment, with their own health, and even with existence itself.

On a personal note, Carole enjoys the abundant sunshine of New Mexico and very much likes dragons.

Great Ayni!

Charts and LifeWeaving Books are available at
AyniLifeWeaving.com or Amazon.com.
Visit www.AyniLifeWeaving.com for updates, new charts and tips for the
LifeWeaving system.

Printed in Great Britain
by Amazon.co.uk, Ltd.,
Marston Gate.